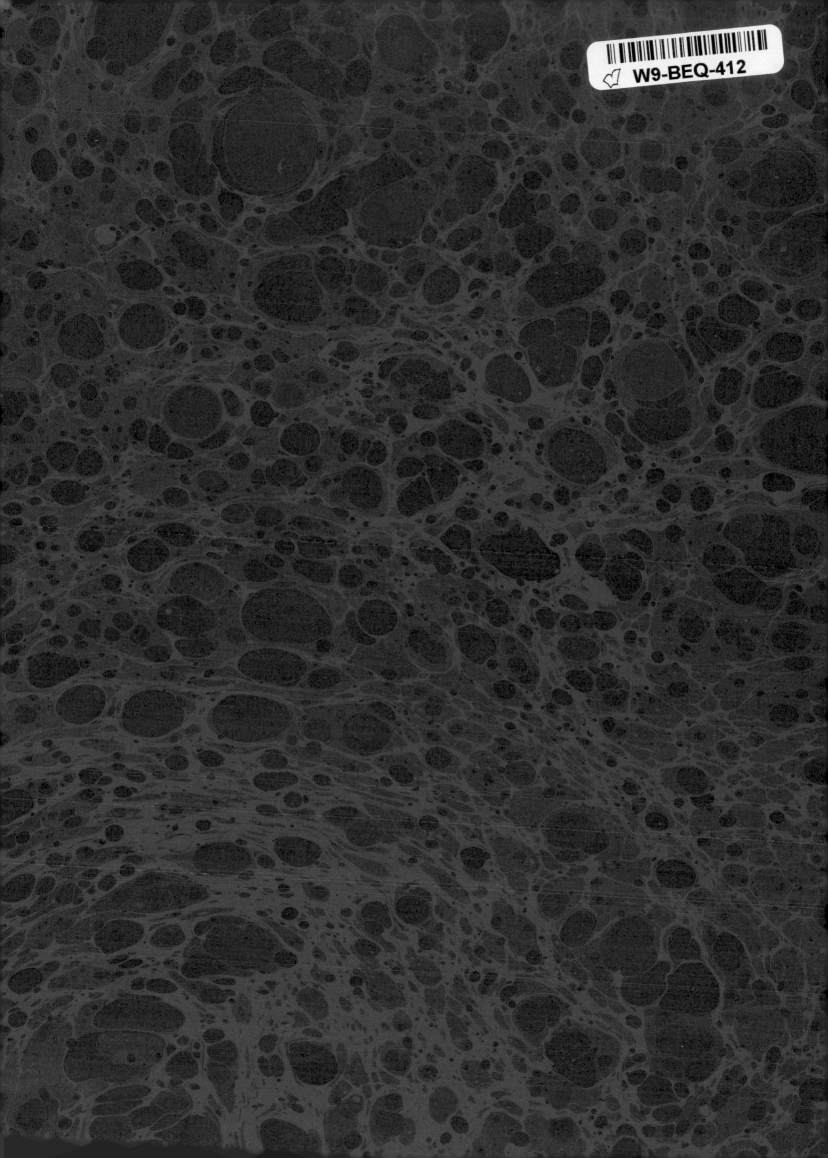

The Enchanted World

THE LORE OF LOVE

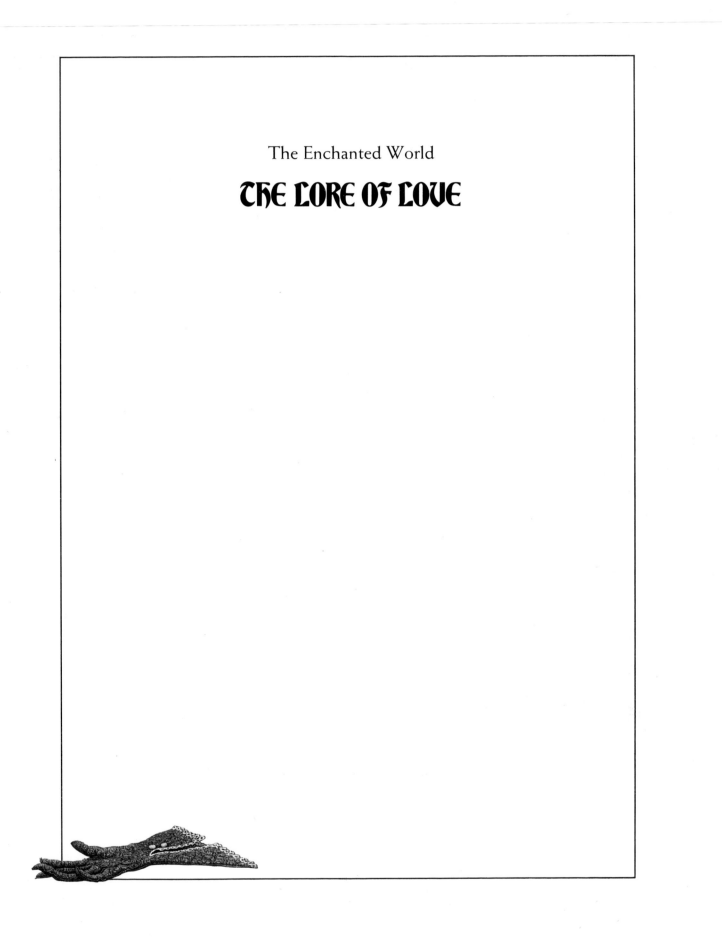

The Enchanted World

THE LORE OF LOVE

by the Editors of Time-Life Books

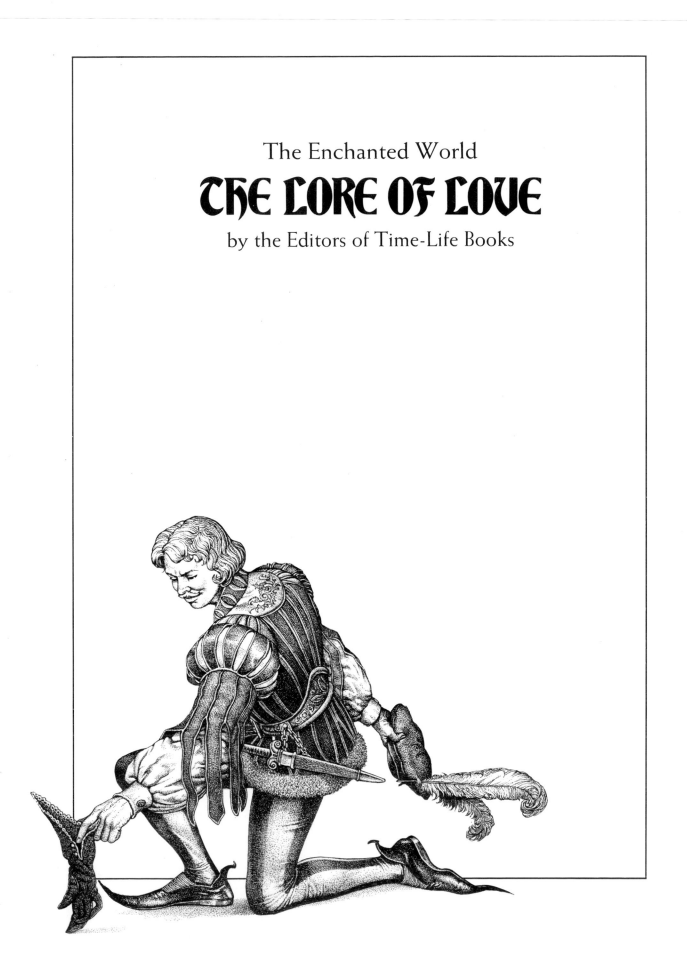

The Content

Chapter One

Destiny's Playthings · 6

◆

Chapter Two

Blighted Passions · 50

Time-Life Books . Alexandria, Virginia

Chapter Three

True Love Triumphant · 96

Destiny's Playthings

In the old world, when gods and goddesses walked upon the earth and unseen powers shaped the lives of mortal men and women, love was never taken lightly. Fierce or tender, sudden as thunder or slow to bud, it was a force that defied all understanding.

Love engendered dreams and nightmares, begat ecstasy or madness, inspired poetry and bloodshed in equal measure. The human heart was its playground and its battlefield, but few folk were foolish enough to imagine that the human will was its master. Young people passed on charms that would, they hoped, enable them to see the face or hear the name of a future mate. But they knew full well that they had no power to change what was thus disclosed to them.

The old lore recorded how deities directed the course of love to suit their own arcane intentions. But there were other supernatural interventions: curses that imposed their own dark justice, and spirits, beneficent or demonic, that broke all bounds of space and time to bring a destined pair together. No matter how remote the antiquity or setting in which these events took place, the tales had for their listeners a powerful immediacy. Love, in all its terror and delight, swept up the souls of peasants as well as Princes, and anyone caught up in its currents was, for a time, on a footing with the gods.

A Groom for the Sea-Lord's Daughter

Beneath the Aegean Sea, claimed the Greek storytellers, lay a kingdom of mystery and magic, peopled by mermaids, monsters and its own subaqueous nobility. The ruler of this realm was Nereus. Although he had long since been supplanted by Poseidon as supreme deity of all the world's waters, Nereus' powers of prophecy were still formidable. On one occasion he used these faculties to foretell the fate of the most beautiful of his own daughters, the Nereids, and thus helped to avert a tragedy of misplaced love that could have threatened the gods.

It was Nereus' fame as a seer that once brought Poseidon himself to seek his predecessor's guidance. Cleaving a path through the waves, which, like good servants, made way for their master, he dived to the sea bed, startling schools of glinting tuna and shoals of sardines. He found the venerable sea-king celebrating the birthday of his youngest daughter, Thetis. Poseidon was received with all due honor, and Thetis herself came to wait upon him. Her beauty so entranced him that he had no appetite for the pink flesh of the oyster or the wine of the sea grapes. Instead he stared, bedazzled, at the nymph who offered them.

Diaphanous robes moving with the current, starfish curling around her toes, the nymph fixed him with the light of her sea-green eyes. The god had never seen a fairer creature. He barely glanced at her sisters, all beauties in their own right, when they danced in her honor.

As Poseidon watched her, his desire grew. Nereus did not need his gifts of prophecy to see what was happening between the Lord of the Sea and his youngest daughter. The King's craggy features grew severe as he observed them.

When at last the dancing stopped, Nereus called Thetis to him and placed a crown of pearls on her head. The sea-spawned circlet was her dowry. Raising her bowed head, Thetis looked up at Poseidon. Their eyes caught, and the enchantment was complete.

Rising, Poseidon announced that he intended to marry Thetis. He expected no quarrel from the nymph's father. When the old King dared to object to the match, Poseidon's fury made the crabs scuttle for the safety of their caves as the sea bed shook. Nereus asked Poseidon to listen to his vision of what lay in store for Thetis before he decided to marry her, but the headstrong Olympian refused. Wiser, if less powerful, than the younger god, Nereus trusted in time to solve the problem and promised that if Poseidon waited for a year and a day, he could make Thetis his bride.

Poseidon had to accede, but visions of the nymph haunted him thereafter. Whether she had used the sea's ancient magic to enthrall him or whether her own beauty had been enough, he was spellbound. Even in the sun-drenched palaces of the empyrean, where the great gods and goddesses banqueted on nectar and ambrosia, her laughing face came before his eyes, making him insensible to all that went on around him.

At one such feast, a dangerous subject arose. Quick-tongued Hermes, the fleet

Enraptured by the charms of the sea-king's daughter Thetis, the god Poseidon watched the nymph receive her father's blessing. He resolved to claim her as his bride.

8

9

When Poseidon brought word of Thetis' beauty home to Olympus, the highest of
all the gods resolved to see her for himself. Shifting into an eagle's shape, Zeus found
her dancing on the seashore and resolved that he, not Poseidon, should possess her.

messenger of Olympus, and ill-favored Hephaestus, blacksmith of the gods, began to debate the relative beauty of the goddesses. Their discussion soon became heated. All present took sides, advancing the cases of their own particular favorites. The ladies in question did not scruple to argue their own good points to the assembly. The rivalry among them was deep rooted. Soon Hera was angry, Aphrodite petulant and Athena appealing to her ever-indulgent father to settle the matter in her favor.

Zeus, anxious to avoid the problem, turned to Poseidon and requested him to speak his mind. The sea-god astonished the company when he said that the most beautiful being in creation was not a goddess but a nymph. The goddesses, sure of their superiority, laughed at Poseidon for being as moonstruck as any mortal fool: It was well known that the sight of a nymph drove human men mad with love.

Poseidon then painted a picture of Thetis, describing her beauty as she danced on the moonlit seashore. The goddesses were not convinced by his description, but the lustful heart of the master of the gods was warmed, and his own interest in the nymph aroused: Lord of fertility, Zeus perceived it to be his obligation to mate with the fairest females, mortals or divine.

The next night, Zeus secretly left Olympus and assumed the form of a sea eagle. He ranged high over the waves, searching for the Nereid's haunt. Against a background of gleaming white sands and moon-dappled water, he spied Thetis dancing. Zeus landed on a nearby rock, watched for a few moments, and lost his heart to the graceful nymph. He returned to Olympus and announced that he wanted her for himself.

Poseidon protested that Thetis had already been promised to him by her father, Nereus. Like two dogs fighting over a bone, the great gods argued. In their anger, the very rock of Olympus began to shake and thunderbolts to fly about over the heads of the immortals.

Just as war threatened to break out between the two brothers, Themis, goddess of justice and daughter of Mother Earth, arrived. The fray was stilled as the gods and goddesses paid her homage. Themis was privy to the secrets of past and future, and she revealed the sea-princess's destiny to the assembly: Any son the nymph bore was fated to be more powerful than his father.

The import of the message was not lost on the brothers. If sired by an immortal, such a child would overthrow the gods of Olympus. Faced with such a disastrous prospect, both Zeus and Poseidon agreed to curb their lust.

The company now considered Thetis' fate. While she remained unmarried, she was a danger, for she might become the bride of one of their fiercest enemies, the giants, who had once nearly defeated the gods in battle. Any son greater than one of these awesome sires would be an intolerable threat indeed. The goddess of justice therefore advised them to marry Thetis to a mortal so that her children would be destined to die like all men.

A youth named Peleus was chosen for the honor of becoming Thetis' husband. The son of a King, he had been unjustly exiled, rescued by the gods and sent to safety in the forest where he lived with the centaur Chiron. There the wise centaur taught the youth all he knew, while Peleus waited patiently to see what the gods had in store for him.

After a visit from Hermes, the Olympian messenger, Chiron sent Peleus to gather yellow sea-poppies at the full moon: His pretext was the need for them in some healing salve. Approaching the shore, Peleus was drawn forward by the sound of musical voices and saw a group of young maidens dancing in a circle on the strand. One nymph—Thetis—was lovelier than all the rest. He watched, fascinated, dizzied with desire. A pause in the dance found him face to face with her. She gave a startled cry, then turned and fled into the sea.

The centaur was not surprised when Peleus returned brokenhearted and without the poppies he had been sent to gather. He informed Peleus that the nymph he had seen and now loved had been chosen for him by the gods. But to win her, he would have to undergo a test. The next night, as she danced on the shore, he was to catch her and hold her fast, without letting go, no matter what happened. Peleus, his body hardened by a life of hunting and wrestling, readily agreed, thinking the slender nymph no match for him. As soon as Thetis appeared, Peleus, more in love with her than ever, caught her in his arms and held her tightly. But then the ordeal began.

The maiden's beautiful face turned into a mask of fury. Her fair skin sprouted black fur, her lips stretched and widened into a snarl, her pearly teeth lengthened and sharpened into fangs, and her nails, now claws, dug into him savagely. From her throat came the menacing growl of a panther as she writhed in his arms, struggling desperately for her freedom. The panther's lashing tail wrapped around his leg, then transformed itself into a cold, constricting snake. The reptile vanished, replaced first by a searing column of fire, then by a roaring waterfall, and then by a sea eagle that churned the air with its wings. Peleus held fast. At last the nymph's powers of metamorphosis were exhausted and she returned, defeated, to her own form.

He was, she told him, the first mortal ever to win a nymph as a bride. Only because the gods had ordained their match had he been given the strength to subdue

A prophecy warned that Thetis would make a dangerous bride for any
deity, so the gods chose mortal Peleus to wed her instead. To win her, he was
compelled to hold her fast through a series of monstrous transformations.

her. They passed the night in one another's arms. The mortal could not gaze long enough at the nymph's face, nor breathe deeply enough of the salty perfume of her skin and hair. As Peleus gently stroked her graceful limbs, Thetis told him of the ways of her people and her life under the waves.

When the dawn lit the sky, Thetis asked Peleus to agree to a single condition before their marriage. Because she was a sea-goddess of ancient lineage, he must never treat her as mortal husbands treated their wives—never speak harshly to her, touch her roughly, nor dare to command her. The goddess in her would not tolerate it. The punishment for any infraction would be swift and final—Thetis would disappear to her father's kingdom for all time. Peleus gave his word.

Before traveling with her lover to Chiron's cave, Thetis stopped to pick some of the yellow poppies that Peleus had been sent for and had forgotten in his ardor. Now there was truly a need for the centaur to concoct a healing ointment: Peleus was bruised and battered from the ordeal he had undergone to win Thetis for his bride.

Chiron greeted them with congratulations. All the gods and goddesses would arrive that evening for the wedding feast. As the first marriage between a god and a mortal, it merited their presence. Mortals and immortals had, of course, met and mated with one another before this time. Zeus, using various subterfuges, had dallied with many a human maiden. To Leda he had appeared as a swan, to Io as a cloud, to the virtuous Alcmene he had approached in the guise of her husband. His passion, though always fruitful, was transitory. Never before had a goddess and a man been joined in lawful matrimony to share one life and one fortune.

The immortals had arranged all the conditions most favorable to a union. January, called Gamelion by the ancient Greeks, was the month ruled by Hera, goddess of marriage. She bestowed special gifts on those who, like Peleus and Thetis, wed under her protection.

Beneath a full moon, traditionally a harbinger of good fortune to nuptial rites. Peleus and Thetis purified themselves by bathing in the pure crystalline waters of a forest spring. Then they entered the centaur Chiron's torchlit cavern to await the guests.

As wood nymphs showered them with fruit and nuts to ensure a fertile union, lions and wolves clustered around the bride's seat. Rabbits, squirrels and field mice scampered around the cave showing no fear of the now-docile carnivores. All paid homage to Thetis. A veil hid her face, protecting her from any evil spirits that might venture to interrupt this festive night. Beneath the gossamer fabric of her headdress glistened the crown of pearls that was her dowry and her birthright from her father Nereus.

From outside the cave came the first faint strains of a divine melody. The animals stopped frolicking. Peleus assumed a regal bearing as he awaited the arrival of the gods who had given him his heart's desire. Zeus came first, then Hera. She bestowed a saccharine smile upon Thetis, her anger at the nymph seemingly forgotten. The trials Thetis was likely to endure as the wife of a mortal man and the mother of his children would be as great a punishment as Hera could wish to bestow on the woman who had so nearly stolen her husband.

Lyre-plucking Apollo and his twin sister Artemis, the virgin huntress, came next, accompanied by the goddess Peitho: All three were patrons of marriage. Without gentle Peitho's aid, no match could succeed, for she ruled the delicate art of persuasion by which two souls were able to live as one. The other deities trooped in and took their places on the thrones Chiron had made ready for them.

All was in readiness. With a few words, Poseidon gave the child of the old sea-king to the handsome young mortal. Now that the marriage was celebrated, the gods and goddesses could rest secure that their hegemony would not be threatened by any son that Thetis might bear.

But one figure stood aside thoughtfully. Nereus, drawn ashore from his undersea realm, had known Thetis' destiny from the start and had realized the threat that fatherhood would pose to Poseidon. Impassively he had waited on the workings of fate in the contest between the sea-god and Zeus, and its happy resolution in the marriage then taking place.

Yet he did not join in the merriment around him. Cursed with clairvoyance, Nereus was doomed to foresee even in joyous times the miseries that lay ahead. While the other guests gazed only on a young couple radiantly in love, he divined, as if in a dream, the anxious parents they would become, tenderly nursing the hoped-for son that would indeed one day be theirs. The boy would grow into a man of might as the Fates had decreed, a youth whose beauty of mind and body would charm all those he would meet. All this Nereus foresaw, yet he did not smile. For he knew too that the son's name would be Achilles, and that all the care and devotion of a doting mother would be insufficient to save him from a grim death in the flower of his days among the horrors of the Trojan War.

To celebrate the union of the mortal and the nymph, beings from every sphere of existence converged at the nuptial feast. Gods and goddesses, centaurs and satyrs, birds and beasts—all came to do the couple honor.

The God of Marriages

In China, so the storytellers averred, every union between a man and a woman was ordained by the immortals. Once the god of marriage had tied an invisible red thread between the feet of prospective partners, no force in the world could snap it. But one tale from the T'ang dynasty told of a man who attempted to confound his matrimonial destiny.

Wei Ku, the hero of the story, was an ambitious young man who had sailed through the examinations into the civil service, and looked forward to an illustrious career among the elite of the Empire. Though Wei Ku's origins were humble, he was confident that his prospects would obtain him a rich and well-born wife. But it was his misfortune to be an orphan; in the days when all marriages were arranged, a man without parents was handicapped in the search for a bride.

When he was twenty-six, the prospects of marriage suddenly seemed to brighten. On Wei Ku's behalf, a friend entered into promising discussions with a senior colleague who had a beautiful daughter. Wei Ku's credentials delighted him. The only topic left to discuss was the delicate matter of the dowry.

The night before the critical meeting, Wei Ku could not sleep for the thumping of his heart. He rose while it was still dark and made for a nearby temple to pray for his friend's success. Arriving just as dawn was breaking, he was surprised to find he was not alone. On the temple steps sat a frail old man immersed in a book. Wei Ku looked over his shoulder and glimpsed a strange, spidery hand. Wei Ku's scholarly education had taught him to recognize every one of the forty thousand characters in the Chinese script, but he could not read a word of this page. Politely he asked the old man what language he was reading.

The old man glanced up at Wei Ku and said it was the writing of the underworld: Surely his interlocutor had seen it before? Then he peered more closely and chuckled to himself: At first he had not realized that Wei Ku was a mortal. At the hours when he visited the earth, the stranger explained, only spirits were normally at large. Aghast at finding himself in conversation with a being from another world, Wei Ku asked the old man his title. "The god of marriage," was the answer. Wei Ku's glance fell again on the great book in the old man's lap. The tome, explained the sage, recorded every marriage on earth—those that had taken place and those yet to be celebrated.

Wei Ku fell to his knees and begged to learn whether or not his marriage negotiations would succeed. Obligingly the god turned to the appropriate page in the book. He shook his head. The discussions were destined to break down that very day. Wei Ku would indeed marry, but not for another fourteen years; his future wife was still only three years old. Wei Ku was appalled at the prospect of such a wait, but curious too. Who was this three-year-old with whom he would at last share his life? The god of marriage offered to show him the girl.

They walked through narrow streets toward the market. By now it was light

Wandering in temple precincts at the hour of dawn, a young scholar met an old
man perusing a volume inscribed in an unknown script. The stranger introduced
himself as the god of marriage; his book named every mortal's destined spouse.

and the traders were setting out their wares. At the noodle stall, a rotund cook was boiling a pan of water. Cloth merchants were unrolling their samples, and peasants in blue tunics were arranging their meager produce—a dozen eggs, a few vegetables, a bag of surplus rice. Suddenly, the god of marriage stopped in front of a ragged old woman setting down her bundle. The young official realized with horror that a grubby infant was clinging to the woman's skirts. Was this destitute child his future wife?

Wei Ku begged to be released from his fate and allowed to wed his colleague's daughter. But the god tapped his book significantly, then opened a leather bag he carried to show Wei Ku a tangle of red threads. One of those threads, he declared, joined Wei Ku to the child, and there was nothing to be done about it. With that, he vanished into the crowd.

Later that day, Wei Ku's go-between disclosed that he had withdrawn the offer of marriage to their colleague's daughter on account of her paltry dowry. Hearing the god's first prediction come true, Wei Ku felt trapped. He determined to act to thwart his unwelcome fate.

That same evening he went to the roughest tavern in the city and hired an assassin to do away with the child. At dead of night a few days later the man returned to claim his reward. He showed Wei Ku his dagger, still wet with blood. Wei Ku was stricken with remorse, but the deed was done. As the years slipped by, he thought about it less and less.

He still tried to find a wife, but every attempt ended in failure. It was not until

To show the young man his future bride, the god took him to a marketplace and pointed out a grubby toddler dressed in rags. Ambitious for a match that would further his career, the scholar was appalled.

Wei Ku was forty, a senior adviser to the government of Hsiang-Chou, that his efforts were at last rewarded. Wei Ku's bride, Wu, just seventeen years old, was a ward of the Governor himself. Following custom, the couple did not meet before their wedding day. Wei Ku first set eyes on Wu when she was carried across his threshold in a red marriage chair, wearing a red silk gown embroidered with dragons, her face invisible beneath a veil.

All through the wedding rituals, Wei Ku had to restrain his impatience to see his new bride's features. Together they bowed to Wei Ku's household gods, then to the ancestral tablets. At the wedding table they paused to eat pieces of two sugar cockerels and dried fruit, symbolic of fertility. Then they pledged one another with goblets of wine and honey tied together with red thread. At the sight of the red thread, Wei Ku blenched, suddenly reminded of the terrible incident from his past. Had he really succeeded in snapping the skein of destiny?

He had to grant that the god of marriage had correctly predicted the age of his bride and the time that would elapse before he wed. But that, Wei Ku reflected, must be coincidence.

When the newlyweds had drunk the honeyed wine, the bridesmaids removed the bride's veil to reveal a ravishingly beautiful young woman. A golden comb held her shining hair in place, and a silver headdress hung low over her brow.

At last Wei Ku and Wu were left alone. They reclined together on the bed and he stroked his bride's face with gentle fingers. She lay quietly, until he made to lift off her headdress. At that, she recoiled. Only after many caresses and whispered endearments did she relent. Wei Ku removed the ornament and started at the sight of a gray scar stretching across his bride's forehead. Gently he asked how the injury had come about. Wu told him her history.

Her aristocratic parents had both died in an epidemic when she was only three years old. After a few months she was sent to live with her uncle, the Governor of Hsiang-Chou, who brought her up as if she were a daughter. But in the confused interim before her uncle adopted her, there was nobody to care for Wu except her nurse. This good woman had kept herself and her tender charge alive by selling vegetables in the market of the city of Sung. Wu could dimly remember the hunger and cold she had suffered. But those hardships were nothing to the sheer terror of the incident that had marred her loveliness.

Out of the market crowd one foggy evening had loomed a ruffian wielding a knife. She could still see his pockmarked face and the look of grim determination in his eyes. But even as he lunged at her, his expression had softened into something like compassion. His change of heart had come too late to stay his knife, which gashed her brow. But, concluded Wu, although she had been within an inch of death that day, some mysterious force of fate had saved her. Wei Ku stroked the scar, trembled, and clutched his destined bride to his heart.

Wielding a dagger, a hired assassin stole into the market. He was commissioned to deflect destiny by murdering the child the gods had chosen as the scholar's wife.

Maidens' Questions

From the earliest eras of recorded time, young girls sought to learn what they could about their future husbands with the aid of love divination. The bizarre rites they performed aimed to summon up the name, profession, whereabouts, even the physical appearance of the men they would one day marry.

Certain times and seasons were propitious for such tender necromancy. Midnight, for instance, was a visionary hour when, in silence and solitude, the bounds of the normal might blur. Certain days, too, were auspicious, among them St. Valentine's Day, May Day and Midsummer Eve. In late January, the Eve of St. Agnes—patron saint of virgins—was intimately associated with love; girls would mix flour, water, eggs and salt to bake a dumb cake, so called because it had to be prepared in absolute silence, then eat it before going to bed to induce dreams of their future betrothed.

Oneiromancy—foretelling the future through dreams—was one of the most common types of love divination. Other forms used magic-imbued aspects of the natural world—fruits, birds, flowers—to call up the image of the beloved in a mirror, or even to make him appear in person. If a girl had a specific suitor in mind, there were tests she could apply to gauge his ardor: A hazelnut placed on a grate might catch fire, signifying passion, or else crack—a sure sign of faithlessness.

Messages written on the wings of birds

A young girl could learn what trade her husband would follow by taking note of the first bird she saw on St. Valentine's morning. The blackbird, with its somber features, indicated a cleric, the jaunty robin a sailor, and the shimmering goldfinch a rich man. But the girl greeted by a woodpecker would never marry.

Footsteps on the path to matrimony

A two-leaved clover, placed in a maiden's right shoe, was a potent agent of divination. The first man she chanced to meet on walking out would either be her future husband or bear the same name.

Preparing a meal for a future mate

A maiden who, in silence, prepared a feast on Christmas Eve could lure her future husband to her hearth. Leaving the table laden and the kitchen empty, the girl concealed herself nearby and waited for the sound of footsteps. If a man appeared and ate the supper, he would marry her within the year. But such dabbling in love magic during the winter, when the forces of darkness were most powerful, could bring misfortune. From her hiding-place, a young woman might catch sight of a monster with burning eyes devouring her handiwork, signaling that she was doomed to marry someone who would make her life a misery.

A nocturnal sortie to the churchyard

Churchyards, resting-places of the dead, harbored potent magic. To walk around the church twelve times at midnight would give a girl a vision of her future mate. A Welsh servant lass, looking for her lover this way, met her employer. Thinking him real and not an apparition, the girl blithely told her mistress of the meeting. The older woman paled with fear, for she believed in magic. Within the year she had died, and by the next the servant was the widower's wife.

Perfumed rites that conjured reveries of love

A rose blossom plucked on a Midsummer Eve and laid beneath a maiden's pillow gave off a nebula of dreams along with its sweet scent. The face and form of the dreamer's future husband would grace her sleep and stay with her when she arose, allowing her to recognize him when they met in their waking lives.

Invoking a husband in a looking glass

A woman could glimpse her future partner in a mirror with the aid of an apple and a comb. First, she had to impale slices of the apple on a knife. Then, standing before the glass, she combed her hair with one hand while holding the knife over her left shoulder with the other. Her destined spouse would come into view, seeming to reach for the fruit.

A Love Forgotten

There was a time in ancient India when the gods and goddesses roamed the earth, when mortals visited the celestial spheres and the course of human love was vulnerable to the intervention of higher powers. Magic and curses, the whims of divinities and the malice of demons could all impinge on mortal unions, drawing lovers together or driving them apart.

Storytellers recounted the tale of two young lovers, King Dushyanta and the lovely maiden Sakuntala, whose lives were shaped, torn asunder and transformed by divine intervention. Sakuntala's father had been a sage whose pious acts of asceticism had been rewarded by the gods with an abundance of fantastic gifts—the ability to create worlds and to kindle stars, to become invisible and to live forever. But the sage's powers changed him from a worshiper of the gods to a rival. The divinities then sought to stop his spiraling ascent to godhead by deflecting his mind from piety to lust.

Stung by the love-god's darts, wooed by a nymph's smile, the old man fell from grace, and the union between nymph and sage produced a child. For reasons the chroniclers did not explain, the nymph abandoned the newborn girl in the forest. Birds protected her from monsoon storms, shielding her with their wings and warming her with their feathers, until she was rescued by an old hermit who took her to raise as his daughter. Nurtured in a sacred grove, Sakuntala grew to be a maiden of perfect physical and spiritual beauty. Her days were spent soaking up wisdom at her adoptive father's feet and tending to the needs of the creatures of the forest. The flame of life was sacred: No animal could be slaughtered for its meat, no insect killed for its noxious sting. When Sakuntala was almost grown, her adoptive father departed on a journey in search of spiritual enlightenment; Sakuntala remained in the peaceful forest world.

To this idyllic place came the King Dushyanta in pursuit of a stag. The stag melted into the undergrowth, leaving the King alone in a canopied bower. A deep serenity filled his heart as he listened to the sounds of the birds, the music of a stream and the murmur of voices chanting the sacred names of the gods. Putting aside his weapons and armor, Dushyanta went in search of the holy man whose sanctum he had penetrated.

By the side of the brook, the King encountered not a venerable and wizened sage but a trio of young girls—Sakuntala and her maids—filling their jugs with water. Hidden by the foliage, Dushyanta admired their beauty. The leader of the three looked up from her labor and her dark eyes met his in a look of such simplicity, honesty and modesty that the King was captivated. Lowering her eyes, she murmured a welcome to the stranger and offered the sweetest fruits to refresh him.

The air of the grove became filled with the scents of spring, the dust of pollen, the love calls of birds and the amorous chatter of monkeys. Whether this signaled the presence of the god of love or the birth of passion between Dushyanta and Sakuntala, the storytellers did not say. They spoke instead of the

Deep in a forest, an Indian King watched a lovely maiden and her two companions fetching water. As his eyes met the girl's, a bond was forged that would bring the pair both joy and anguish.

King's growing certainty that Sakuntala was the woman he wanted for his wife. With each word that she spoke, with each expression that animated her face, Dushyanta became more and more enamored. When he learned of her true parentage and knew that her rank matched his, he took her hands and asked her to be his Queen. Tentatively returning his caresses, Sakuntala admitted that her heart, too, had been kindled by desire.

Pledging their souls to one another, the pair were bound in wedlock. A marriage between two such high-ranking mortals needed the sanction of neither priest nor parent. Love alone sufficed. Taking seven steps forward, each step symbolizing one of the seven boons of marriage, Dushyanta and Sakuntala thus sealed their promise. Pressing his hand to her breast, Dushyanta vowed to take her heart into his, and to lead her forward throughout their lives together.

Dushyanta remained at the hermitage for several days before his duties called him back to the palace. Before he left, he gave Sakuntala his ring. The emerald was engraved at its center with the symbol of royalty, alerting all who saw it that the wearer was a member of the royal household. Promising to send for her, Dushyanta rode away in his chariot.

Sakuntala spent the next days wandering through the grove, lost in thoughts of her beloved. Sitting by the brook where she had first met Dushyanta, she turned his ring around and around on her finger and sighed with longing. An elderly stranger came up behind her and waited impatiently for her to offer him the food and water that was the due of any visitor. As the moments passed, and Sakuntala dreamily ignored him, the old man shook with anger and his lips formed a dreadful curse: The person she was remembering would have no memory of her.

Hearing his voice, the young girl was roused from her reverie and thrown into a panic of fear as she recognized the man. He was a master of curses, before whose imprecations even the gods trembled. Tears streaming down her cheeks, she begged him to forgive her and to recant his oath. Shaking his head, he told her that the curse was more powerful than its maker and could not be recalled. But her contrition moved him to a proviso: Her husband would remember her on seeing the ring. Showering him with thanks, Sakuntala made the visitor welcome.

When her adoptive father returned, Sakuntala told him of her marriage and of the child who now stirred in her womb. The sage gave her his blessing and sent her to join Dushyanta.

Dushyanta's palace teemed with suppliants and beggars, holy men whose only possessions were a single garment and a bowl, Princes whose trumpeting elephants stirred up clouds of dust that obscured their riders and covered the crowds in grit. All awaited an audience with the King. Sakuntala was both proud of her husband's power and fearful that, guided only by her retinue of unworldly monks and sheltered maidservants, she would not find him in the midst of it. Pushing forward, she reached the King's deputy and requested an audience with Dushyanta. A smile played about the courtier's lips as he regarded the beautiful woman whose anxious eyes and rounded belly spoke all too clearly of her plight. A victim of her womanly frailty and some man's wiles, she was only one of many seeking the King's help in righting a misfortune. But his pity turned to annoyance when she avowed that she was the King's wife and insisted on an immediate audience. Just as the chamberlain was about to refuse, Dushyanta himself appeared. He acknowledged Sakuntala with the courtesy of a well-mannered stranger and began to move on through the crowd.

With a cry of despair, Sakuntala threw herself at his feet and begged him to acknowledge her as his wife. Dushyanta looked down at her with incomprehension, as Sakuntala feverishly recited the details of their courtship and marriage. No spark of recognition entered his dark eyes, merely a glint of distaste for a liar. Recalling the old man's curse, Sakuntala held out her hand to show Dushyanta the ring and restore his memory.

As she did so, a cry of grief escaped her lips, for the ring had gone. Perhaps sorcery had removed it, or a thieving beggar; or maybe it had slipped off as she bathed in a pool along the way. The King's love was as lost to her as the fatal circlet. With a sigh and a sharp word to his courtiers for having allowed the nameless woman to annoy him, Dushyanta moved on, his heart filled with sadness at the wicked ways of women.

Sakuntala was led sobbing from the courtyard by her attendants. Standing outside the palace, she was overcome with misery and stretched her hands out to the heavens, begging the gods she had worshiped all her life and the mother she had never seen to come to her aid. In a flash of light, her prayers were answered: Sakuntala disappeared.

When Dushyanta heard what had happened to the strangely beautiful woman, he felt sure that her words had been the work of sorcerers and was glad that he had not heeded them. Still under the power of the old man's curse, the King thought no more of her for many years.

His forgetfulness ended when the missing ring was presented to him by a poor fisherman, who had found it in the belly of a fish. The sight of the emerald instantly revealed to him the identity of the woman he had dismissed so long ago. Filled with horror and remorse, he ordered the fisherman rewarded and the country scoured for his wife. The search was fruitless, for Sakuntala's prayers had brought her mother to her rescue. Sakuntala and her child now resided in the heavenly palace of her nymph parent.

Assuming the robes of a penitent, Dushyanta neglected the duties of kingship as he mourned his wife. The corridors of the palace grew quiet, the gold in the treasury gathered dust, the food collected as tax or tribute rotted, the King's horses idled in their stables, fat and lazy. Nothing could interest, rouse or amuse him.

Dushyanta remained entombed in grief until a war broke out between the gods and the demons. The divinities called

upon all mortal Kings to come to their aid. Throwing off his lethargy and calling his startled servants to bring his armor and weapons, grown thick with dust and stiff from disuse, Dushyanta stepped into the chariot sent by the god Indra.

In the battles that followed, Dushyanta fought side by side with the gods against the ranks of demons. Demon blood reddened the sky, and the clash of steel deafened the mortal world as the war between the forces of good and evil drew to a close. Silence returned only when the last of the demons was vanquished. Above the clouds, now washed clean by Indra's rain, the gods could be glimpsed riding victorious in their chariots.

Dushyanta headed home to his kingdom in Indra's chariot. The charioteer, perhaps on the orders of the god himself, suggested that they break their journey at a cloud-built palace high in the empyrean. The King came upon a celestial garden that rang with a child's laughter. The sound drew him like a magnet, and soon the King found himself gazing into a face whose features mirrored his own.

Filled with wonder, Dushyanta looked about the grove, hoping to spy the boy's mother. At that moment, Sakuntala came forward, and their long separation was ended. The ring that had once been the token of their love and later its bane, first spurring, then clouding, memory, was put away for all time. A love such as Dushyanta and Sakuntala's, shaped by the gods, needed no other symbol than the small boy who stood beside them.

Separated from his wife before the birth of his son, the King at last
came upon the boy in the garden of a nymph's heavenly palace.

31

The Cursed Embrace

Love, for those fortunate enough to find it, was a joy and a blessing, but the storytellers warned against complacency. The path to the nuptial altar was strewn with perils. Even when all circumstances were auspicious, fate or frailty could intervene to deflect the expected happy ending. Such was the message conveyed in the old German tale of Liba and Guntram, a couple who seemed, at first, to bask in the sunlight of good fortune. In the tradition of their time and class, they were chosen for one another by noble parents, interested in the establishment of a mutually advantageous alliance. Yet from the young people's first encounter, there was a natural sympathy between them, and love grew with every meeting.

Liba was the daughter of the Lord of Falkenburg, and it was to his castle, high on a beech-clad hill overlooking the Rhine, that the knight Guntram rode through the golden days of autumn for the betrothal. The ceremony was as binding and elaborate as marriage itself, with a gathering of parents and close family in the castle chapel, solemn prayers and the exchange of vows.

The customary interval of forty days before the marriage should have been a time of gentle courtship, of walks in the garden and whispered confidences. But Guntram was urgently summoned to attend his lord on a mission to the court of Naples. It would take six months, so there would be no wedding until spring.

With promises of undying devotion, the lovers parted. Guntram hung from his lance a stocking that Liba had given him, and twined a lock of her hair in his hel-

met. In Italy, Guntram's passion for Liba grew ever stronger. When his mission was completed, the slow return journey filled him with impatience. Once the entourage had crossed the formidable mass of the Alps and reached the German border, he gained his lord's permission to ride ahead; he could accomplish the remaining miles more swiftly alone.

Three days' journey from Falkenburg, he was overtaken at dusk by icy rain. A wan light, dimly perceived through a mass of trees, promised refuge. But when Guntram reached the source of the light, it was only a half-ruined castle.

An aged porter opened the door to his knock. He led the knight into the shadowy hall, murmuring a welcome on behalf of his absent master, made a promise of supper, and withdrew. A feeble fire did little to warm the weary traveler, and while he waited for his meal, he began to wander about the room peering at the dark pictures lining the walls. They depicted only saints in agony and personifications of death in awful guises.

At the far end of the chamber, heavy curtains shrouded another painting. He drew them aside to reveal the likeness of a beautiful woman strangely seated by an open grave. Her pale green eyes seemed to follow him about the room. Feeling that her gaze was inescapable, he was glad to cover her portrait once more.

The servant entered with a tray of food and drink. When Guntram had supped, the porter led him along cobwebbed corridors to a distant bedchamber. A gauzy veil hanging from a hook, its once-brilliant colors now faded and dusty, and a pair of high wooden pattens, too small for a man, told Guntram that the chamber had once been a woman's. Though he was exhausted, he was restless and, pacing about, he discovered a door that led into a small, empty room. This he judged to be the lady's wardrobe. The scent of lavender hung in the air. It was more pleasing than the musty tang of the bedchamber, so when he retired to bed, he left the door ajar.

He woke from a dreamless sleep as a distant bell struck midnight. His opening eyes were troubled by a shaft of light that slanted across the canopied bed. Raising himself on one elbow, he looked into the next room. A woman stood in its center, and the light seemed to radiate from her. She sang softly under her breath. The flowing hair and haunting look were familiar. She was the woman in the portrait. Her outstretched arms tempted him, but as he reached out his hand to throw back the coverlet, the sight of his betrothal ring reminded him of Liba. When he looked up again, the stranger was gone.

Next morning, the lover who only the day before had been in such a hurry found reason to delay his departure. His longing for Liba was overwhelmed by a feverish desire to see the unknown woman again.

All that day he searched through ruined rooms where swallows nested, and in gardens given over to rabbits and foxes. Weeds sprouted from a tombstone set into the chapel floor, but the inscription was still legible—"Pray for me, but fear my glances." It echoed in his mind like a

Taking shelter in a half-ruined castle, a German knight came upon a portrait depicting an unknown lady beside an open grave. The image perturbed him, as if he had some premonition of the part the lady would play in his fate.

At the moment of uttering his marriage vows, Guntram felt the grasp of ghostly fingers.

Then he saw that another, dreaded face had replaced the countenance of his promised bride.

warning; still he searched but he failed to catch even a glimpse of the woman.

Eventually, darkness came, and after a time of wakefulness he dropped into a restless sleep, only to be aroused as midnight chimed. Once again light streamed from the adjacent room; once again the woman stood in its center. Guntram rose and, moving toward her, asked who she was. She only shook her head and beckoned once more in a gesture of invitation. This time, he stepped into her arms and embraced her. After a moment, she drew from her finger a heavy gold band and placed it on his. Then she was gone.

Early next morning, Guntram, bewildered and shamed, left early. Hastening downhill, he met a peasant toiling upward and paused to ask why the castle was so neglected. The peasant told him of the lady who had lived there long before. Beautiful and coquettish, Etelinda had drawn many suitors to her side. But her demands on them were such that none had stayed to wed her, until one came who declared that he would do anything in the world if only she would love him.

With a cruel smile, she challenged him to stand unarmed at a crossroads on Walpurgisnacht, a time when wise mortals kept indoors, for it was then that witches gathered for their great sabbat.

The youth's bloody limbs were found the next morning, scattered over the highway. Some said he was the victim of wolves, but his grieving mother knew it was the work of witches, and she cursed Etelinda. The girl sickened and, nine days later, died in agony. Folk whispered that her spirit knew no peace, but wandered the world until she found a man who could resist her gaze. All who succumbed to her embrace were doomed.

Appalled, Guntram urged his horse on toward Falkenburg. He completed his journey in a daze of despair. But, once in familiar surroundings, and warmed by Liba's welcome, the knight began to believe that true love might banish the ghost's evil influence. The ring was no longer visible on his finger, though he seemed always to feel its weight.

A fortnight later, guests gathered for the nuptials. Accompanied by the music of viola and flute, the wedding procession wended its way to the church. Peasants lined the route to doff their caps as Liba, clad in fur and cloth-of-gold, rode past on mule-back, followed by Guntram on a white palfrey.

But at the very moment of exchanging vows, something terrible took place, something that would have been beyond belief if priests and worshipers had not been there to witness it. When he spoke the words that would join him to his bride forever, Guntram looked down to discover that the hand he held was not Liba's. The frigid fingers of a specter gripped his own. And Etelinda's calculating green eyes, not Liba's candid blue ones, gleamed from the upturned face.

The apparition, seen by all, lasted but a moment. Then Liba stood beside him again. But Guntram never knew, for at the sight and touch of the phantom bride he had fallen into a delirium. Nine days later, he joined her beyond the grave.

A Rendezvous
in Dreams

In the innermost court of an Arabian palace, where the splashing of many fountains confounded the ears of spies, a King, troubled by the cares of state, paced sleepless through the night. He summoned one of his concubines, a celebrated storyteller, to divert him.

She told a tale of love and magic to drive away the demons of the dark. So strange was her story that it did what she could never do—slipped out through the seven guarded gates of the harem. In time, it became common currency in all the souks and seaports of the East. Yet it was a tissue of absurdities and improbabilities, a chronicle of lovers who would never have met if a pair of capricious spirits had not meddled in human affairs.

The narrative began in a kingdom somewhere in the heart of Asia, where the steppes rang with the voice of a royal father, raised in anger against his son. The Prince Camaralzaman, roared his exasperated parent, was an abomination

in the eyes of heaven, for he refused to fulfill the destiny to which he had been born: to marry and beget an heir. Prospective brides had been brought by caravan along the routes of silk and spices, but he would not consider them. Dancers had been summoned and slave-girls purchased to kindle the fire in his loins. But he spurned them all in favor of his lute and volumes of poetry.

Persuasion having failed, the King resorted to threats and then to punishment. Camaralzaman was taken out of the capital to a ruined city on the plain, graveyard of some forgotten race, and immured there in a crumbling tower. It was the King's despairing hope that the nocturnal chill, the croaking of ravens and the attentions of ghosts might persuade his stubborn son to a change of mind.

In the tower, Camaralzaman was allowed no visitors; his food was sent up daily in a basket. If he suffered, he gave no sign of it. Lacking his lute, he sang;

Manipulated by unseen beings, a Princess who had forsworn love became enamored of a stranger.

deprived of his poetry books, he composed verses of his own. But his father was right in one respect: The tower was indeed haunted. It was well known that the demons known as jinn loved abandoned buildings and lonely countryside. They might ride the winds to visit others of their kind in the farthest reaches of the earth, but they were loyal to the places they claimed as home.

The jinni of this tower took a certain pride in his princely tenant and boasted of Camaralzaman's gifts and graces to other members of the unseen world. Another spirit—a female of the species known as *ifrit*—claimed she knew a mortal maiden who equaled and perhaps even surpassed Camaralzaman in beauty. This prodigy was a Chinese Princess named Badoura who, like Camaralzaman himself, had incurred her father's displeasure by refusing to marry, and was now a prisoner in a disused wing of his imperial palace. For the sake of experiment, the two spirits decided to bring the mortals together and place them side by side so their charms might be compared.

The jinn were masters of the air, adepts in the mysteries of rapid movement. The uncountable miles between Camaralzaman's home and China could be crossed in a single instant. In the depths of night, when their powers were strongest, the two spirits conveyed the Princess Badoura, all unwitting and fast asleep, to the ruined tower where Prince Camaralzaman lay.

Each in turn was nudged awake by their invisible captors. Badoura, roused first, gazed for a long time at the sleeping stranger, who looked so like her he might have been her twin. She reached out a finger to trace the curve of his cheek and the line of his lips. But before she could wake him by her touch, the jinn conjured her back to sleep again.

Camaralzaman, when his time came, was enraptured by the lady beside him. He cried aloud that he had never had a dream as sweet as this before. Eager to take some token of his bliss back into the bleak world of his waking, he slipped a jeweled ring off the unknown lady's finger and exchanged it for one of his own. Then he was sent to sleep again, and Badoura covertly carried back to China.

The next morning Badoura and Camaralzaman woke up in their separate places of confinement to find themselves alone. The Prince called for the slave appointed to serve him in the tower and demanded to know who had brought the beautiful

The jinni and the ifrit—a female spirit—argued over the relative merits of their human protégés.

visitor to him and where she now was. Bewildered, the slave denied all knowledge of the woman; he swore that he had been on guard by the door all night and that no one had passed him.

At this, Camaralzaman flew into a rage. Seizing the trembling man by the hair, he threatened to kill him instantly if he did not tell the truth. Breaking free, the slave fled in terror to the King's palace to report this latest twist in the young Prince's condition, and to stammer out to the ruler his fear that imprisonment had turned his master's mind.

The King was deeply concerned at the news, and hurried to the tower to talk to his son in person. Camaralzaman, who assumed that the woman he had seen had been sent by his father, just as many others had in the past, poured out his love for her and showed the King the circlet, elegantly carved with unfamiliar symbols, that he had taken from her.

Mystified, the ruler swore that he had no knowledge of the girl; but he grieved for the affliction that her disappearance had evidently brought upon his son. So saying, he ordered the young man's release forthwith and took him back to the palace. Camaralzaman,

struck down by despair, collapsed and was carried to his bedchamber.

In distant China, the object of his passion suffered torments of her own. Neither the King nor his counselors were convinced by the presence of the ring on Badoura's finger. They had long suspected that the girl was mad—why else would she refuse to marry? Now, with these ravings about a handsome stranger, their fears were confirmed. Not all the purgings, powders and pinpricks of the court physicians could rid her of her delusions. She was imprisoned in her quarters once again, and the King announced that any man who could cure Badoura's malady should have her as his bride.

But one of the palace doctors believed the Princess's story. Marzawan was the son of Badoura's old wet nurse, though his skills and scholarship had elevated him far beyond the rank he was born to. Sharing the milk of a single mother, he and Badoura loved one another like brother and sister. In a secret interview with his patient, he looked carefully at the foreign ring on her finger. He recognized the symbols upon it, he said, as the insignia of a royal house in a kingdom far to the west. Promising Badoura that all would be well, he left the palace, taking with him a miniature portrait of the Princess.

When Badoura declared her love for the foreign Prince, her father dismissed her as a hopeless madwoman.

For months there was no word from him. Then Badoura heard from her maids that Marzawan had returned to the court. He brought with him a stranger clad in the gown of an astrologer. Here, announced Marzawan, was a wizard of the west, steeped in the occult wisdom of India and Egypt. He and he alone held the secret for curing Badoura.

When the magician entered the Princess's chamber she cried out, for this was the youth she had met in her dream. He, like Badoura, had been deemed insane. When Marzawan arrived with Badoura's portrait, the Prince was restored to his senses. He had commanded the doctor to take him to the lady at once.

The reunited lovers were sequestered for many hours. What questions, endearments, vows and caresses passed between them the chroniclers did not reveal, but the couple emerged together to bow before the King and ask that he fulfill his promise and marry Badoura to the man who had healed her. The wedding was hasty, the King only too glad to see his difficult daughter depart on the journey to her spouse's homeland.

The nights of the honeymoon were passed in a silken tent, pitched in flowery meadows or on palm-fringed shores. The newlyweds did not speed their journey, choosing instead to prolong its pleasures. One morning, encamped in a wilderness halfway between their two countries, Camaralzaman kneeled beside Badoura, caressing her as she slept. As his hand strayed among her silken garments, he encountered something he had never noticed before—an amulet of chalcedony, carved with occult symbols. Curious, he unpicked the knotted cord that held the talisman and carried the gem out of the tent, so that he might examine it more closely in the light of day.

What happened next was so extraordinary that it must have been a new intervention by the jinn who had first brought the lovers together. A bird—and no ordinary bird, for its eyes glowed red like beacons—swooped and snatched the amulet from Camaralzaman's grasp. The bridegroom did not know the object's significance, but he imagined it was precious to his Badoura, perhaps some charm inscribed by priests to keep her safe from evil. Fearing his bride's anger at the loss of her talisman, he set off in pursuit of the winged thief.

Badoura woke to find both bridegroom and amulet missing. Camaralzaman's possessions and clothes were all as he had left

The magician who came to cure Badoura's delusions proved to be her mysterious lover in disguise.

them. A cup of sherbet, half consumed, stood waiting for him to lift it to his lips again. A book of love poems lay open on the pillow. She did not imagine for a moment that he had left her willingly, but as the day drew on, she lost all hope of finding her spouse, her amulet, or any explanation of their disappearance.

For the sake of safety, Badoura dressed herself in Camaralzaman's cast-off clothing: Princess she might be, but in this alien wilderness she was as vulnerable as any other lone female. In the folds of her robes, she concealed the jewels that formed her dowry. Then she set off along a road that led to the sea. She asked the few living souls she met along the way if they had seen Camaralzaman. But the answer was always no.

In this world without maps, Badoura had only hearsay to tell her how far she was from home. No one she spoke to recognized the name of Camaralzaman's kingdom, and though a few folk had heard of her own native China, they shook their heads when she asked the way there. By patient questioning, she learned of a cargo ship bound from a nearby harbor to an island whose name she knew. From the Isle of Ebony had come the dark carved tables in her father's throne room. If she could reach the place where they were crafted, she would be safely on a trade route to her home.

Purchasing her passage with a handful of sapphires, Badoura arrived at the Isle of Ebony. Still in male disguise, she announced herself as a Prince from China. The Sultan of the island pressed his hospitality upon this distinguished traveler. So charmed was he by the decorous manner of this youth—and so impressed by his royal pedigree—that he offered his only daughter's hand in marriage. No boat was expected to sail to China for a year or more. Badoura, who had quickly grown into a friendship with the maiden in question, calculated the risks and probabilities, then squared her shoulders and accepted the proposal.

On the wedding night, Badoura's secret could not be kept for long but, as she had hoped, the bride's reaction was not dismay but gales of laughter and a promise of complicity in sustaining the deception. Absorbed in the pleasures of one another's company, Badoura and the Princess hardly noticed the passage of time. When the next boat laden with ebony set sail for China, Badoura was not aboard.

The Sultan had chosen to retire from the throne to a life of meditation and

While Badoura slept, her bridegroom discovered a talisman concealed within her garments.

prayer. Following ancient custom, he conferred the crown upon his daughter's spouse. Badoura proved to be a wise and kindly ruler, and found that she liked the taste of power. There was little incentive to go back to China and live out a drab existence in her father's court as the abandoned wife of Camaralzaman.

One morning, a merchant called at Badoura's palace with a gift for the new Sultan and his Queen: a jar full of ripe golden olives from a village on the mainland, famed far and wide for the succulence of its crop. Badoura dipped her hand into the vessel to sample the delicacies. She frowned and dug deeper, then pulled out a small, hard object that had been concealed among the fruit. It was stained and slippery with the oily juice of crushed olives, but she recognized it at once: It was the talisman that had vanished with Camaralzaman on their honeymoon.

Bounding from her throne, she grabbed the merchant by the collar and shook him. She demanded to know the olives' source. He named the village, and she struck him once; he named the grove where the olives were picked, and she slapped him a second time; he named the gardener who had handed over the jar, and she let him go. She commanded the trader to sail again to the olive grove. The gardener was a thief, perhaps even a murderer; he was to be captured and brought to her. Before the week was out, the ship returned.

Badoura had prepared a dungeon filled with implements of torture so that she might interrogate the prisoner and learn the fate of Camaralzaman. But when her intended victim was dragged before her, she let out a cry of amazement and ordered the captive's release.

Camaralzaman stood before her, his skin tanned by the sun, his hands hardened by toil, but otherwise unchanged. Badoura sent everyone from the chamber and revealed to Camaralzaman that she too was not what she seemed. It took many hours before Camaralzaman finished his account of his own trials and travels. If he had not before suspected the hand of some jinni or demon in his relations with Badoura, he was now convinced of it. The events that took him away from her—and those that brought them back together—not only strained all credibility but defied any material explanation. He told of his pursuit of the bird that had snatched the talisman, and how the creature had lured him into a trackless wilderness. For many weeks, he

At the Sultan's command, a band of sailors went ashore to capture the supposed thief of the amulet.

lived on what he could kill or gather, until finally he made his way to a settlement, and from there was put on a road to the coast. There, an old gardener, owner of an olive grove, had offered him food and shelter in exchange for his labors.

A pampered Prince he might have been, but in the olive grove he had learned how to work hard and take pride in it. One day, while he tended the trees, he heard a rushing of wings above him and a bright object struck him on the forehead—a carved piece of chalcedony dropped from the beak of a bird flying overhead. Camaralzaman recognized it as Badoura's amulet and knew instantly that he was still a plaything in the hands of unseen powers. He placed the gem on a cord around his neck and began once more to live in hope.

One day a merchant ship arrived at the tiny harbor. Camaralzaman hoped it might carry him toward his own country, but it was bound only for the Isle of Ebony. Its captain had come to purchase golden olives to present to Ebony's new Sultan and his Queen. Camaralzaman clambered up and down ladders, reaching out to pluck the most perfect specimens from the trees. Only when the ship had sailed did the Prince realize that Badoura's talisman had fallen from his neck. For days he searched every inch of the olive grove without success, sick with despair. When the sailors came back and put him in chains, he offered no resistance. He did not ask why they had apprehended him, nor did he care. Life had lost its meaning until this present moment when, against all probability, he found himself standing before his beloved once again.

Badoura, accustomed by the duties of kingship to swift decisions, proposed a course of action. She was overjoyed to see her husband, but she had no desire to leave the Isle of Ebony or its Queen. There was, she said, no law in this country against a man having more than one wife. If Camaralzaman would take the Queen of Ebony as his second spouse, Badoura would doff her masculine disguise, and the trio could rule the Isle together. Badoura had no doubt that they would do so in peace and harmony.

As she proposed, so it was done. No celebration in the island's annals equaled in grandeur the wedding and Camaralzaman's coronation, neither in the length of the procession, nor the size of the sacred elephants, nor in the quantity of golden olives consumed at the nuptial feast.

The second marriage of the Queen of the Isle of Ebony was celebrated with extravagant pomp and ceremony.

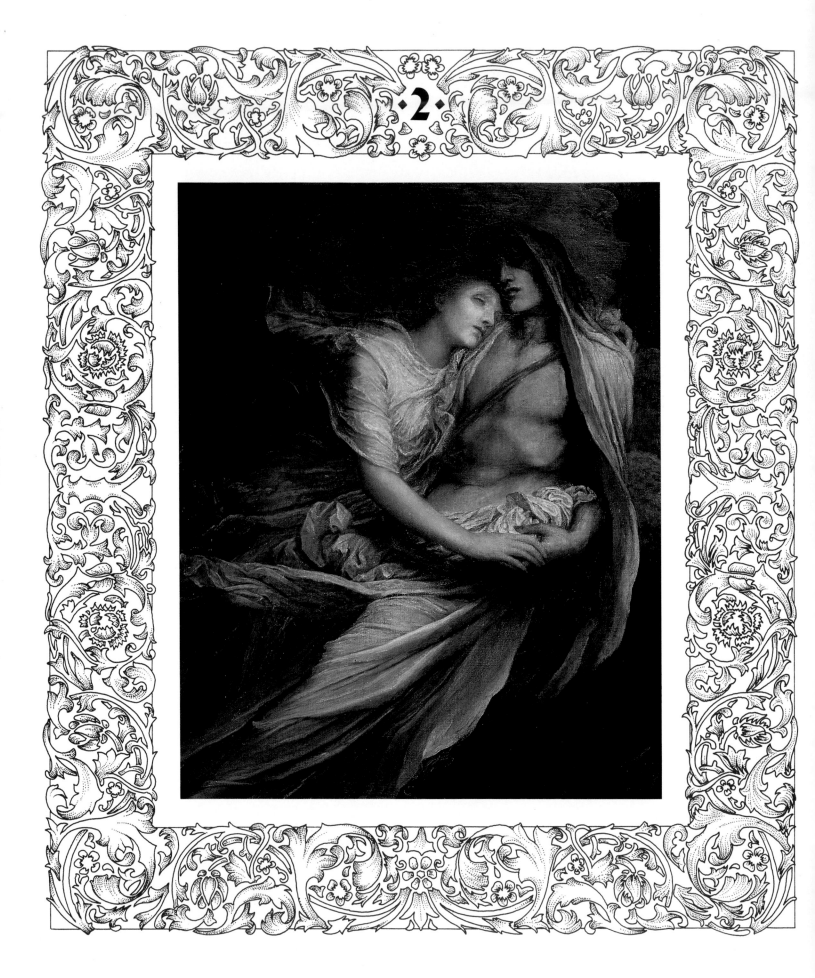

Blighted Passions

Even for fortunate couples, the power of love could be frightening in its intensity; but when things went awry, the results were terrible. Just as there was no rapture greater than that of the fulfilled lover, so no fate was more fearful than that which fell on those whose passion was thwarted.

Sometimes the enemies of their joy were divine, for the gods could take a perverse delight in setting snares and entanglements in the path of amorous mortals. More often, though, the agents of destruction were human and of the victims' closest kin: mothers, fathers, brothers. Such was the case when suitors unwittingly contravened any of the unwritten social rules of coupling, the web of restrictions and taboos woven by men in a vain attempt to channel the uncontrollable torrents of desire. Interdiction could, in fact, be a positive incitement; the lure of the forbidden was always strong, and the one man or maiden whom social convention or parental prohibition proscribed as a partner often became the target of secret desire.

When that happened, doom threatened. If ill fortune attended the couple, the road to satisfaction might be forever barred to them. In that case, the star-crossed wretches who had fallen foul of destiny would be driven down ever-darker ways shadowed by regret and despair, their only exit to suicide or madness.

An Aztec Couple's Reunion in Flames

In a lost century, under a younger sun, there flourished in the arid valley of Mexico the great Aztec city of Tenochtitlan. Its ruler was an elderly Emperor whose authority was absolute: Laws were made or unmade at his whim, and brutal execution was the penalty that attended his slightest displeasure.

One of the old man's hardest decisions directly affected his closest kin. He had a daughter named Ixtaccihuatl—Ixtla to her friends—whose raven hair and dark, impenetrable eyes would have won her a place in the secret imaginings of every young warrior. But for all her charms, her father had decreed that she should not marry. His reasoning was simple. In the course of a long reign, he had learned to trust nobody and to confer no real power on any individual. Authority, mused the Emperor, would inevitably devolve upon a son-in-law; and he was not prepared to sacrifice his guiding principle of government for his daughter's happiness.

Of all the Emperor's warriors, one man had the audacity to risk his master's wrath by falling in love with the girl. His name was Popocatepetl, and he was a Jaguar Knight—a soldier of the imperial bodyguard. The uniform of wild ocelot skin he wore proclaimed his elite status at court. But, whenever Ixtla appeared at the palace, her father's arm resting on her shoulder, Popocatepetl could only dream.

It happened that one summer, when the heat baked the red earth of the valley as hard as stone, the Emperor fell sick. This was the moment the nation's many enemies had long awaited.

Like condors at the kill, they swept down from the mountains flanking Tenochtitlan and circled around the city walls, crowing for blood. Wanting orders, the warriors crowded into the palace to await their Emperor's command.

At last the old man appeared and disclosed a desperate strategy. Every soldier, he declared, must drink deeply of the spirit of Tezcatlipoca, the ancient god of war. The warrior who proved bravest in battle would be richly rewarded, for he would win the hand of Ixtla, heiress apparent of the Aztec empire.

Every warrior fought valiantly, fired with desire for the Princess. But the soldier
whose feats repulsed the invaders was he who truly loved her, Popocatepetl.

A swell of murmured amazement ensued, then all at once the palace courtyard erupted into a riot of jostling bodies. It had taken a terrible crisis to reverse the Emperor's decision, but now Ixtla was available, and the path of eligibility for suitors plainly marked out. Men ran back to their homes, already ululating the chilling Aztec battle cry, and feverishly dressed themselves with bells, feathers and bracelets—the caparisons of war.

Only Popocatepetl remained where he stood, transfixed, watching Ixtla help her father down the long corridor to his bedchamber. Almost swallowed from sight by distance and shadows, the Princess at last turned and looked at him. He thought he saw a glimmer of love in her eyes. Then she was gone. His heart racing, the young warrior marched from the

courtyard and up onto a high battlement. Scowling down at the enemy through the gaping jaws of his helmet, Popocatepetl steeled himself to fight harder than he ever had before. Then, drawing his obsidian machete, smooth as polished glass, he strode out to meet the foe.

The atrocities and deeds of reckless courage done that day long fueled the ritual storytellings of the Aztecs. Blood flooded from so many wounds that it trickled under the city gate and into the marketplace. As was their custom, the women wailed to the divinities to protect their menfolk, and poured ashes on their heads to blacken their tears. And in the sanctuary of her father's palace, Ixtla prayed hardest of them all.

Eventually, the cacophony of battle receded, then ceased altogether. The women left off their keening and waited in suspense. At last, there came a knocking at the gate, and a small party of Aztec soldiers entered. The Emperor himself, supported by Ixtla, staggered out into the night to meet them. Which way had the battle gone? he demanded. A wonderful victory, they answered—the enemy was annihilated. And this triumph was the handiwork of which warrior? pressed the Emperor. Of Popocatepetl, the Jaguar Knight, chorused the soldiers. Always he was ahead of his comrades, surging into the hottest blaze of battle, his machete slashing a bloody trail through the enemy ranks; always calling out, firing them to fight harder. How tragic it was, some cunning warriors added, that this noblest of men should have met such a

After his beloved was tricked into taking her own life, the sorrowing Popocatepetl
built a pyramid to her memory. Bearing a flaming torch to the summit
of another pyramid, he became one with the rock, an ever-burning volcano.

horrible death, for the enemy, in a last, desperate stand, had surrounded Popocatepetl, fallen upon him like pariah dogs on a lion and ripped his body to pieces.

Though nobody in the city knew it, the soldiers were lying, for Popocatepetl had been wounded, not killed. As they spoke, his strength was reviving. He had bound up his wounds and, like the natural commander that he was, had decided to let his exhausted soldiers rest before returning to Tenochtitlan. By spreading false stories of his demise, his rivals for the hand of Ixtla hoped to claim the girl for themselves. But their conspiracy was shattered by the Princess's despair.

Some say that the daughter of the Emperor died by her own hand; others, more fancifully, claim that she willed herself to death, having lost all reason to remain in this world. Whatever the truth of it, Ixtla's lifeless body was that night discovered lying on the floor of her bedchamber, curled like an autumn leaf.

Early the next morning, Popocatepetl marched into Tenochtitlan at the head of his weary army, bounded up the palace steps and claimed the Princess for his bride. At the sight of his champion, the Emperor buried his face in his hands and left it to the women to tell him of Ixtla's death only hours before.

Popocatepetl's wrath was terrifying. Drawing his scarred and splintered machete once again, he stalked through the streets of the city and dragged out the warriors who had cheated him; without a word, he killed them all. Then, it is said, he faced the crowd that had followed and guided him from house to house, and commanded them to build a massive funerary pyramid outside the city walls.

Every able-bodied man and woman set about the task, and soon the monument was finished: sheer and white, crowned on top by a golden bier. Popocatepetl carried the body of his beloved to the summit and laid it there. He then called to the people below to build another, higher pyramid nearby, so that he might stand atop it and see forever his lost bride. When this too was made, Popocatepetl took a crackling pinewood torch and slowly scaled the steps, not once looking back. He never returned, and no Aztec ever dared follow him. But the torch he held for love of Ixtla blazed for all time. For the warrior became one with the rock of the pyramid, and the pyramid itself became one with the earth. The volcano called Popocatepetl, the Smoky Mountain, burned perpetually for snow-capped Mount Ixtaccihuatl below.

Recipes for Romance

In the ages when people pinned their hopes on magic, they believed that love, that most mysterious and powerful of emotions, could be sustained by charms and philters. Ancient manuscripts described a whole litany of spells and a pharmacopoeia of potions and unguents claimed to incite passion in the breast of the indifferent. The weird medicaments and bizarre brews may never have worked (unless it was to nauseate or poison the beloved), but they said much nonetheless about the hopes and dreams of lovers.

Some of the strange formulae adopted the homeopathic principle of like breeding like. Trying to stimulate desire, suitors would tempt their loved ones with oysters, renowned for their fecundity. Or else they would melt a heart-shaped piece of wax before a flame, believing their action would soften the heart of the one they yearned for.

Others thought they could win love by secretly acquiring loose hairs or nail clippings from the hoped-for lover, then mixing them with their own. The resulting charm would be hidden under the chosen one's pillow, or placed near the doorstep of her home or on a path she was accustomed to follow.

Most common of all the types of love magic were herbal remedies not unlike those prescribed by conventional doctors and healers of the day. Such ingredients as vervain, elecampane and basil were often mentioned in the recipes; but no plant was reputed as potent as the mandrake, whose oddly shaped root, sometimes resembling the human body, was considered to be a great love-promoter.

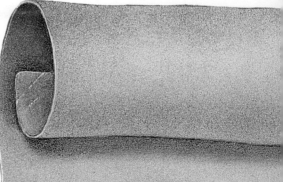

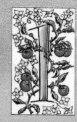

The fruitful and evergreen orange tree, a symbol of marriage since the days of ancient Greece, provided a remedy for unrequited love. Wise folk said that if its fruit was thoroughly pricked with a needle and held under a man's arm overnight, it would inspire passion in any woman who ate it.

Some sorcerers reveled in using unlikely ingredients in the mixtures they purveyed. One charm designed to keep a woman's love was said to contain marrowbone from a wolf's paw, mixed with ambergris and powdered cypress. Delicately scented with perfume, the philter was supposed to enchant the woman with its odor.

Orchids, it was said, were the food of the lascivious satyrs. Some claimed that a vigorous young root, powdered and sprinkled over food, could make mortals frolic like the goat-footed revelers. Many women, though, found to their sorrow that the charm's effects diminished once the marriage vows had been pronounced.

 Witches concocted for gullible customers improbable amalgams alleged to rouse overwhelming passions in the heart of anyone who ate them. One recipe included the dried and ground liver of a pigeon and the brain of a blackbird. The resulting powder was sprinkled over the loved one's food.

 A faithless man could be brought to heel, it was claimed, by a spell woven in roses on Midsummer Eve. Three blossoms had to be hidden in the small hours, one under a yew tree, one in a new-planted grove, and one under the girl's pillow. They were left for three nights, then burned, firing the man's dreams with images of his lover.

 Two kinds of magic could be used in concert to tie down a wandering lover. Earth dug from one of his footprints and placed in a pot stopped him from roaming. And to keep him faithful for the future, girls were advised to plant in the pot loyal marigolds, whose heads turn daily to follow the path of the sun.

 Another potion guaranteed a woman's constancy by ensuring a place in her dreams. A lock of her hair had to be burned to ashes, which were then sprinkled on the frame of her bed and held in place with honey. Stuck fast, the cinders were meant to keep the hopeful lover before the woman's eyes, even as she slept.

 One unpleasant potion mixed a dove's heart, a swallow's womb, a sparrow's liver and a hare's kidney, all dried, powdered and mixed with the spellmaker's own blood. Even more difficult than the task of finding the ingredients was the problem of persuading the loved one to consume the philter.

 Even in darkest midwinter, when the trees on which it grew had shed their leaves, mistletoe stayed green. Perhaps for that reason it was always associated with fertility. Merely to stand beneath a sprig of the white-berried plant at the season of the winter solstice and exchange a kiss was thought to foster love.

The stone avenger

From the rainy hills of Galicia to the sunbleached Andalusian shores, Spaniards listened spellbound to the tale of an amorous grandee named Don Juan and his assaults on female virtue. While other men of his time explored the great oceans, braving tempests to redraw the map of the continents and the charts of the seas, Don Juan was quite content to remain at home, navigating from lace-trimmed petticoat to starched farthingale, always one step ahead of his conquests' enraged fathers, brothers and lovers.

But there came a time when Don Juan went too far and seduction led to murder. One fateful night, he disguised himself as the fiancé of the proud and beautiful Doña Ana of Seville. In her dark bedchamber, the deception went unnoticed; too late the lady realized that the man she embraced was an imposter.

Her cries brought her father to her aid. Half-dressed, and with his sword drawn, Don Gonzalo made ready to kill the man who had betrayed his daughter's honor. As their shadows danced on the wall of the bedchamber, the two men rent the night with the clash of steel. Amid the parry and thrust, Don Juan's blade found its mark, mortally wounding his adversary.

Escaping from the palace, Don Juan fled to the countryside. The city and its pleasures were a potent magnet, however, and he soon returned to Seville, hoping that the scandal of Don Gonzalo's murder would by then be stale news. But the plazas were still humming with gossip. Ducking into a church for safety, Don Juan discovered that the shadow of his crime stretched there too. He found himself gazing at a newly completed sepulcher, surmounted by a stone statue of the murdered man. With a sardonic laugh, he reached up to tweak the sculpted beard. Then, with ironic politeness, he invited the effigy to do him the honor of dining with him at its earliest convenience.

That night a hollow knocking resounded through the inn where Don Juan was staying. In the doorway loomed the man of stone. As the servants fled in horror, the statue sat down to dinner with Don Juan. A fine roast chicken grew cold before the silent guest, and the silver wine goblet never touched his lips. But before he rose to leave, he invited Don Juan to sup with him in his chapel the next evening.

For all his vices, Don Juan was a man of courage, and he did not flinch from accepting the statue's invitation. The supper that awaited him in the tomb proved to be a bitter feast: scorpions and vipers washed down with draughts of gall and vinegar. Behaving with exquisite politeness, Don Juan did his best to swallow the repugnant morsels.

When the meal ended, the guest rose to take his leave. But the stone statue seized his hand and held it in a grip that burned like molten metal. Struggling to free himself before his flesh was seared to the bone, Don Juan lashed out with his sword, but the blade passed through the statue as if through empty air. When Don Juan begged for mercy, the statue announced that the time for forgiveness was past. All that awaited Don Juan now were the fires of hell. And the old man's ghost had all eternity in which to savor its revenge.

No one ever found Don Juan's body. Thus it was impossible to ascertain whether he died of the poison he had eaten, of the statue's searing touch, or simply of terror. But the storytellers could account for his disappearance. The sepulcher's lid swung open, they said, releasing white-hot flames and a stench of brimstone and sulfur. Then, with a dull thud that thundered in the dark streets of Seville, it closed once more, entombing Don Juan and his enemy together.

The Pot of Basil

In the days when Italy rang with the high song of the poets, there was a simple tavern tune that for a while enjoyed widespread popularity. From marketplace to cloistered garden, the familiar refrain could be heard: "Who has stolen my pot away?" But few knew the tragedy that lay behind the words.

That tragedy was the story of Lisabetta, whose eyes were like sapphires and whose skin was smoother than the finest silk of Cathay. She lived in Messina, in the home of her three brothers, who were wealthy merchants, ambitious for the fortune and honor of their family. The brothers had not yet found a suitable husband for her and, being mindful of custom and propriety, rarely allowed their sister out of the house. Lisabetta passed her days in the cool shade of the loggia, where she could look down on the teeming street below. Sometimes she would be rewarded by the sight of a noble on a finely caparisoned palfrey, or a fat prelate perched on a mule, querulously calling for way, or sharp-eyed Gypsies watching for the unguarded purse. But Lisabetta was hidden from the world.

One year, as the heat of summer grew and the Dog Star reached its zenith, the three brothers engaged a young clerk to manage their account books. His name was Lorenzo, and the maids spoke in awe of his beauty. At first Lisabetta only heard his footsteps on the stairway or the echo of his voice. Sometimes, if she strained her ears, she might hear the faint scratching of his pen. Finally, she ventured down to the cool, dim counting room where he sat hunched behind an oaken table. He looked at her through the bars of his abacus, unable to tear his eyes away from her face.

Thereafter, an unspoken bond held them together. When strolling through the house, she would stop and linger in the counting room, aware of his gaze, and she would peer with feigned comprehension over his shoulder at the crabbed figures, barely touching the velvet of his doublet and smelling the warmth of his body. One day he thrust the abacus aside and, in a voice that trembled between despair and hope, confessed his love. At first she tried to hush him. Then terrible desire awoke in her, and she responded without restraint. Soon Lisabetta became careless even of the watchful eyes of her brothers, and would hurry each evening through the echoing marble corridors to the room where Lorenzo lay.

It was on one such night that her eldest brother, who had a careful, cat-like tread, saw her slipping into Lorenzo's chamber. Immediately he informed his brothers. They were prudent men and, with the interest of family honor at heart, arrived at a plan that would discreetly solve the problem.

During the days that followed, the brothers showed nothing of their rage toward Lorenzo, but appeared perhaps more convivial than usual. One evening they persuaded him to come out carousing. Lorenzo went with them to a lonely spot outside the walls of the town. Not until they drew their daggers did he apprehend his folly. But by then it was far too late. They stabbed and slashed him until their fury was spent. Then they returned to the house and told their sister that Lorenzo had suddenly been sent away on business.

Every day Lisabetta watched the street for the return of her love. Each time she saw a clerk's cap moving through the crowd, her heart leaped in anticipation. But Lorenzo never came. When she questioned her brothers, they affected surprise. Why, they asked, was their dear sister so interested in the whereabouts of a mere counting clerk?

As the days passed and there was still no sign of Lorenzo, Lisabetta feared she had been deserted. Then, one night, Lorenzo appeared to her in a dream, pale and wild eyed, his body torn with red gashes. He stood before her in the moonlight and begged her to stop her weeping, for he could never return to her. He told her of his murder and described the exact spot where her brothers had buried him. And then the vision faded.

At first Lisabetta suspected some trick of the Devil. Nevertheless, the next day she escaped the vigilance of the servants and ventured out into the street, unattended. Following the instructions given to her in the dream, she made her way to a certain bush outside the town wall and, using her delicate, white hands, began to dig through the dead leaves and moist earth. She soon found what she sought.

She tried to lift the corpse, unable to bear the thought that even death could keep them apart, but Lorenzo was too heavy for her to move. Then, said the chroniclers, she was maddened by her great grief. She brought out her jeweled knife of damascene steel and set herself to sever Lorenzo's head from his body. When at last she had succeeded, she carefully wrapped up the head in her white linen wimple and took it back to the house.

On the cool loggia overlooking the street stood several large, earthenware pots. In one of these she hid the head of Lorenzo, covering it with earth and placing above it several plants of good Salerno basil. As the Dog Star waned, the basil, watered daily by her weeping and fed by the rotting head in the soil, grew luxuriant and sweet.

Her brothers were puzzled by her attachment to the pot and eventually, as her beauty wasted before their eyes, became suspicious. One day they took the pot away to see what it contained. They found the head and recognized Lorenzo. Terrified that the murder would be uncovered, they buried the evidence and hastily fled the city.

As for Lisabetta, when she discovered the theft of the pot, she fell into a fit and then into a fever. However much the physicians bled her, she never ceased calling for her pot of basil, and within a fortnight she died of desolation. But Lisabetta's cry lingered on after her soul had departed, and became the song that told her bitter story.

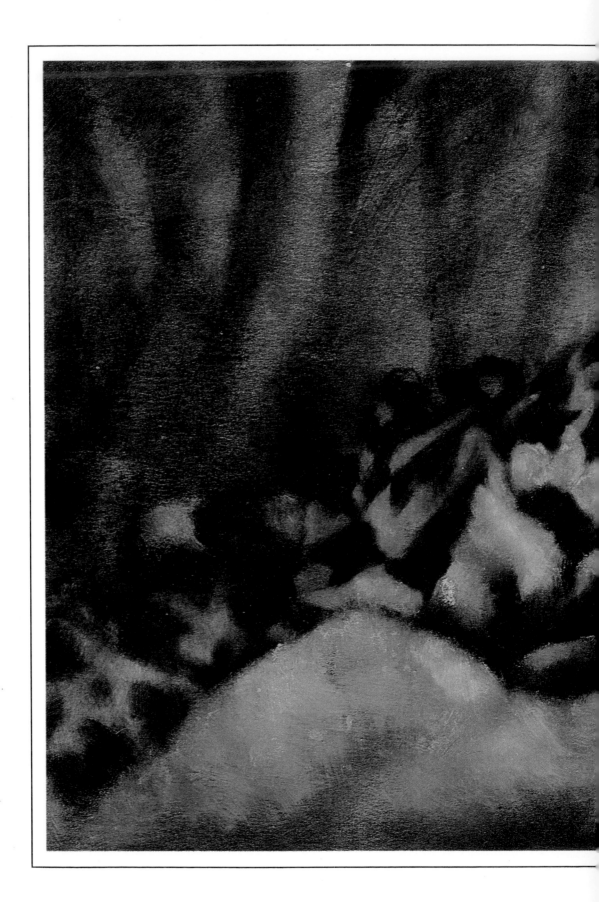

Following instructions given in a dream, the lady Lisabetta found the
corpse of her murdered lover. Unable to disinter the body of her beloved,
she severed his head and spirited it home to mourn over at her leisure.

The Tale of a Demon-Bride

In ancient China, poets told many tales of folk brought to destruction by marrying for love. Sensible young men took heed and let their families choose suitable partners for them. But for a man named Shushuan, who had no parents to guide him, love's temptations proved irresistible.

Shushuan lived in Hangchow, lakeside capital of the Sung dynasty, with an uncle and aunt who had a flower shop close to the city walls. Most days he was busy in the shop from early morning to late at night. But each April, on the Festival of the Dead, his uncle gave him leave to visit his parents' graves and perform the rituals of remembrance. One year, love entered Shushuan's life.

On that day, the clear water sparkled in spring sunshine as the young man made his pilgrimage across the lake to the graveyard of the Temple of the Awakening on the far shore. But the weather soon changed. Performing his rituals as quickly as piety allowed, Shushuan returned to the beach and ordered the boatman to row back to the city.

As the prow was turning toward the waves, a voice hailed them and begged to be taken on board. On the beach stood two young women: a servant, dressed in blue, and her mistress, the loveliest being Shushuan had ever seen, in a mourning gown of white.

Perhaps it was the solitude of the lake, with mist obscuring all sight and sound. Perhaps it was the intimacy of the small boat as the passengers sat, their knees touching, face to face. Whatever the cause, Shushuan was hopelessly enraptured with Lady White by the time the party stepped ashore at Hangchow.

The three companions huddled together against the rain as they walked up to the great white walls of the city. They hurried through the monumental gateway and along the narrow streets, jostled by porters and rickshawmen. Finally they parted outside a grand townhouse, whose roofposts were carved like serpents' heads. And Shushuan felt his whole body tremble when Lady White, to thank him for his kindness, invited him to visit her that evening.

Long before darkness fell, Shushuan, in a torment of desire, knocked at the door beneath the serpents' heads. The blue-robed servant led him into a splendid room. Lady White was waiting. They kneeled together by a low table, and she poured him a cup of rice wine. For several minutes they looked at one another in silence. Finally Lady White spoke.

In a low voice she told Shushuan that she realized he was a poor man, whereas she was a wealthy widow; a great gulf separated their stations in society. But she had fallen in love with him. If Shushuan would deign to take her for his wife, she would give him everything she owned. Before Shushuan could reply, she handed him a small casket that stood by the table. Inside was a stack of gleaming silver pieces. "Go now," she said, "and tell me your answer tomorrow."

Shushuan was so astounded that he made no protest as the maid led him to the door. But as he walked back toward the flower shop, his blood surged at the

A Chinese pilgrim, departing from a lakeside temple, was hailed by two
figures at the water's edge. Returning, he found a lady in white mourning
robes and her handmaid, who were stranded on the shore and begged for his assistance.

very thought of possessing Lady White. When he reached the Imperial Way he broke into a run. Within minutes Shushuan was bounding up the stairs to his uncle's apartment, eager to reveal to his relatives his good fortune.

Shushuan's uncle, though, was a determined foe of sentiment. He snorted contemptuously at his nephew's story, and when he was shown the silver pieces he tested each one with his teeth. They seemed real enough. Then he realized that every coin was brand new, and his expression turned to one of fear. Perhaps they had been stolen from the Imperial Mint? And the penalty for robbery was death. He dragged Shushuan off to repeat his story to the magistrate.

Soon a party of armed guards was standing outside the house with the serpents' heads. No one answered the door, so they broke it down. The building was empty, and there was no sign that anyone lived there. Dust lay thick upon the floorboards, and a loose shutter rattled in the bare reception room. But as the guards turned to leave, a gust of wind blew the shutter open. For an instant it seemed that a woman in white was standing at the top of the stairs in a shaft of moonlight. The guards dashed forward, but the shutter closed with a bang and the apparition was gone. On the floor where she had stood lay a pile of silver coins.

Shushuan spent that night in a damp and miserable cell. The next morning he was summoned before the magistrate, who listened to his story impatiently, then banished him from the city. "If you are telling the truth," he declared, "then the Lady White must be a demon. And there is no place in Hangchow for men who deal with demons!" The guards took Shushuan to the north gate and stood there jeering as the young man trudged away down the road to Soochow.

At Soochow, Shushuan managed to find a job in the flower market. For some weeks he was more miserable than he had ever been in his life. But he made a firm decision to forget Lady White, and by the beginning of summer, when the roses were blooming, he had begun to enjoy life again. Then one day he was on an errand outside the market when a carriage pulled up alongside him. In it were Lady White and her servant.

When Lady White invited Shushuan into the carriage, all his resolution vanished. Once more they were sitting knee to knee. Fiercely she denied all the accusations that had been made against her. She had not been in the house when the guards came, and the silver was her own. She had waited for him fruitlessly on the following day. Now that chance had brought them together once more, she hoped she would not lose him.

Shushuan did not go to the market that day, or the next. When he did return, it was in a sedan chair carried by two porters; and he was wearing a fine silk gown embroidered with golden serpents. He had married Lady White.

The couple lived in a splendid house in the best part of the city. While his wife remained at home, pampered by servants, Shushuan wiled away his time in the

Investigating reports of a crime, the city guards broke into the home of the white-clad lady. They were greeted by an apparition in snowy robes. The figure vanished before their eyes, leaving no trace but a pile of silver coins.

fashionable taverns and teahouses, where he soon made new and wealthy friends.

In time, though, he grew homesick. He dreamed of revisiting the lake of Hangchow, and gazing once more on the white city walls and the glittering tiles of the roofs. When a friend suggested they travel there secretly for the religious festival of the First of the Tenth Moon, Shushuan agreed. They decided to go to the Temple of the Awakening, where he could again burn incense on his parents' graves and sweep their burial mounds.

Lady White looked troubled when she heard of the plan, but she consented to it on two conditions: that Shushuan should not enter the temple, and that on no account should he talk to any monks. Shu-

shuan was content to humor his wife's whims, so he gave his word and the friends set out for Hangchow. When they reached the temple, they found it crowded with visitors, for the monks were displaying all their treasures: silks, tapestries, rare objects of silver and gold. Eager to see these wonders, Shushuan's friend steered him toward the doorway.

Without thinking, the young man stepped inside. Instantly he came face to face with the aged abbot of the temple and the memory of his vow rushed into his mind. He turned and ran, paying no heed to the monk's cries.

Shushuan raced down the path to the lakeside just in time to see a boat nearing the shore. In it were Lady White and her maid, beckoning him aboard. As he stepped into the shallows, a voice behind him called out, "Be gone, demons!" At that, an extraordinary thing happened.

Trapped at the behest of a priest who knew them to be demons, the lady and her servant shifted shape, becoming a white snake and a small blue fish.

The boat began to spin, faster and faster, as though caught in some mighty whirlpool. At last it sank beneath the surface, leaving no trace behind.

Shushuan was gazing open mouthed at the spot where it had been when the abbot grasped his shoulder. Sensing that the young man was in mortal danger, he had followed him to the lake; it was his voice Shushuan had heard. Now he listened carefully as Shushuan stammered out the strange story of his marriage.

A look of concern spread across the holy man's face as Shushuan told his tale. When he had finished, the old monk warned him that his troubles might not be over, for such demons were hard to kill. He told him to return to his uncle's shop; but first he gave him a monk's robe as a disguise lest he be recognized and arrested, and a begging-bowl. The abbot warned him not to let go of this if he should see his wife again.

Shushuan took the monk's advice, and soon found himself back in the street in which he had grown up. His disguise fooled even his uncle and aunt as he stepped into the shop, but their surprise turned to consternation when they realized who he was. "How can you be a monk?" his aunt demanded. "Your wife is here. She said you would be coming. She is waiting upstairs."

Shushuan would probably have fled had it not been for the force that he felt emanating from the holy man's bowl. Trembling, he climbed the staircase to the upstairs room. There he found his wife, a dark glow flickering like flame in her otherwise expressionless eyes.

As the woman flung her arms around him, Shushuan pulled the bowl out from the broad sleeve of his robe and forced it down upon her head. She screamed horribly, but Shushuan maintained the pressure. To his surprise, he found that the bowl was sinking downward, as though his adversary were shrinking. He bent his full weight into the task. Soon the bowl was level with his waist, then his knees. At length he forced it to the floor, and though it continued to move spasmodically beneath his fingers, no sign of Lady White remained to be seen. Her maid, who had come running in answer to her cries, had also vanished.

Clamping a lid on the bowl, Shushuan ran with it back to the temple. The old monk, with due solemnity, recited a prayer of exorcism over it. Then he lifted up the lid's edge. The bowl was not empty. In the dim light inside, Shushuan could make out the forms of a blue fish and a coiled white serpent. "Lake spirits," the abbot muttered by way of explanation, then ordered the bowl and its contents to be buried on safely hallowed ground, deep below the foundations of a new pagoda that was being built.

Shushuan was reprieved by the city magistrate. He spent the rest of his days as a monk in the Temple of the Awakening. Perhaps that was the end of the story. Centuries later, however, the pagoda where the bowl lay buried was destroyed by fire, and rumors spread of a white serpent and a blue fish seen wriggling away from the conflagration.

Vanity's reflection

No bard or troubadour ever sang more poignantly of lost love than the poets of ancient Greece, who told how the gods made cruel sport with the affections of humans.

Among the victims of the capricious Olympians was Narcissus, fairest of mortal youths. With his dark locks and marble skin, Narcissus won the love of every girl who looked upon him. All being available, he was attracted to none, and spurned their advances. Meeting rejection, their love turned to hatred; one embittered maiden called upon Nemesis, goddess of revenge, to make Narcissus in his turn suffer the pangs of unrequited passion.

The goddess answered the girl's prayer. To lead the youth astray, she used the hapless wood nymph Echo, whose fate it was to be able only to repeat the last words of any remark made to her. So it happened that when Narcissus, hunting deer, became lost in the forest and called out for aid, the sole reply he received was his own cry softly reiterated in the nymph's sibilant tones.

Pursuing this gentle music, the youth was drawn deeper and deeper into the woods, until he came to a clearing where water lilies dappled a still pond. There, leaning over the bank to drink, Narcissus finally found an object for his passion—his own reflection in the limpid water.

From that moment on, he knelt besotted beside the pool. Now and again he reached to embrace the perfect creature who looked up at him, but the image would disappear as his fingers disturbed the water. Stricken by unfulfilled love, he wasted away until all that remained of his beauty was the white and gold flower that bears his name. As for Echo, she remained faithful to the young man she had unwittingly led astray; her disembodied voice continued to haunt the forest glades.

Spurning the charms of the girls of Greece, Narcissus finally found an object for his love—

his own reflection in a pool.

By a miraculous transformation, the nymph Daphne escaped the clutches of the love-hungry Apollo.

Thisbe was kept from her lover—but only by a wall's thickness.

Doomed trysts

The arrows of Eros, trickster god of love, were of two sorts. When gold-tipped, they roused passion; if pointed with lead, they deadened it. Sometimes the mischievous boy would use the contrary weapons to set two beings against one another. To avenge an insult, he once enamored the sun-god Apollo of the nymph Daphne, while making her reject his advances.

Through the glades of Olympus the two ran, not in lovers' play but in the deadly earnest of the hunt. Daphne could not long escape; no one was as swift as the mighty Apollo. At the moment of capture, though, she cried to the river-god who was her father, and he stole her from the sun-god's grasp. Her downy skin hardened into bark, her limbs froze into branches. She was transformed into a laurel tree; and ever after Apollo wore a wreath of laurel in memory of her.

When even gods' loves went awry, it was no wonder that the mortal path was harder still; and no human couple were more unfortunate than Pyramus and Thisbe. The poets do not say which heavenly being confounded their fate, but from the start their love was ill starred. Their families, though neighbors, were deadly enemies. The only way the pair could whisper their passion was through a crack in the wall that joined their houses.

Finally, frustration drove them to arrange a tryst in the dangerous woods outside the city. Thisbe was first to arrive, but seeing a lioness prowling nearby, she fled, dropping her shawl, which the beast spotted and mauled. Pyramus, finding the garment stained with blood from the animal's maw, thought his beloved dead. Having no reason to go on living, he impaled himself on his sword. Thisbe returned in time to see him dying; caught in fate's inexorable web, she used the weapon to gain the solace of death.

he Obsession

As rain could make the desert flower, so love in happy circumstances could bring joy even to the hardest heart. But in its darker moods, love could be a devastating force, a fount of ruin. In the barren lands of Armenia there once stood a craggy outcrop, tall, bare and sunbaked, that was to become a silent testimonial to this destructive power.

Some centuries ago, a lone traveler approached it from the east. He was a sculptor named Farhat, and he decided to break his journey at its base. Dropping down his tools thankfully, he took a long draught from his water bottle, then made himself comfortable against a rock and fell asleep.

His dreams were suddenly interrupted by the thrilling of horns and the baying of hounds. Rising hastily to his feet, he found himself surrounded by a throng of richly caparisoned hunters. Momentarily he was enveloped in the warmth of their jollity, and then they were away, racing each other and the hounds across the sprawling plain.

Farhat sank to the ground again amidst the clouds of settling dust and gazed after the hunting party in bewilderment. In all the noise and commotion, one image had impressed itself on his mind and heart. It was a vision of pure beauty—a lady's smiling face that had turned briefly toward him before vanishing like a mirage into the hot plain.

Accustomed as he was to bringing life to cold stone, the sculptor could not help but be moved by beauty, and this was such as he had never seen before. Abandoning his journey without a thought for those who awaited him,

On a journey through a stony wasteland, a sculptor saw a lady riding to hounds. Though she barely glanced at him as she passed by, he surrendered up his heart and soul for love of her.

Farhat became from that moment a man obsessed. Every day he could be found at the same hour waiting by the roadside for the hunt to pass again, hoping for another glimpse of his vision.

He learned to live frugally off the land. For food he trapped small animals, and in the cool of the night he traveled to replenish his water bottle at distant wells. But always he returned at dawn to the same place, to wait for the riders to pass. Sometimes they would come, galloping gaily by, and he would be rewarded for his patience with a careless smile from his beloved, flung to him like a penny to a pauper. Then he would consider all the time spent waiting well lost.

The months passed slowly by, and the desert chilled with the onset of winter. Farhat knew that the hunt would not be riding again until spring returned, but obstinately he haunted the same spot, hoping to see his love once more.

Then one day, the sound of hooves rang on stone, and she was there, accompanied only by a small group of her handmaidens. She reined in her horse and halted in front of the sculptor. To Farhat, she looked lovelier than ever in her long, flowing winter cloak edged with sable. Gazing down at him, she asked why he always waited there. Was he so fond of hunting? She turned to acknowledge the laughter of her entourage.

Suddenly conscious of his own ragged and unkempt appearance, Farhat lowered his eyes in confusion and replied quietly that he waited only in the hope of seeing her pass by. The lady clapped her hands in delight at his answer and turned again to murmur with her attendants. Then she smiled at Farhat. Seeing from his tools that he was a sculptor, she told him that if he truly wished to please her, he must prove his devotion by making her something befitting her station, for she was the Princess Anoush, daughter of the Persian King. Then she lightly pointed up at the barren hill behind him. "There is all the stone a sculptor could possibly need," she said. "Do what you will with it."

As she rode away with her retinue, Farhat pondered on her words. He saw in them an offer of her affections, a promise of future happiness together if he could only form a project worthy of her love. And so a great design began to take shape in his head. He would make her no common statue or monument. Instead he would hew from the rock a dwelling-place, a stately palace where he and the woman who obsessed his soul could spend their days together in love and happiness, as man and wife.

Throughout the long cold months of winter he plotted the site with meticulous care. He took many measurements,

gauged angles and examined the face of the rock for flaws. By the time spring arrived, he knew every inch of the hill as well as he did his own body.

Like clay in the sculptor's hand, the misshapen mound of stone slowly began to take form. By day travelers heard the noise of Farhat's hammer and chisel echoing high up on the hillside and wondered. By night they could see his flickering shadow as he worked by the eerie light of flares driven into the looming cliffs. Word of his strange task passed through the land, and people came from far and wide to marvel at his handiwork.

The months passed into years, and still Farhat toiled ceaselessly on. The power of his love flowed into his hammer and chisel, causing the hard unyielding rock to split and fall away like ice in a thaw. Driven by the beauty of Anoush, he fashioned spacious chambers and lofty halls, magnificent state rooms and splendid stairways. The dead rock sprang to life with carved reliefs depicting the glorious exploits of Anoush's ancestors.

He carved spacious stables for the Princess's Arab stallions, and storerooms for the many rich treasures she would bring with her. Finally he fashioned the peak of the hill into a turret chamber. From it, his loved one could survey all the lands where she used to hunt, as well as the spot where Farhat and she had met.

At length everything was finished, the last pediment hammered out, the final corbel embellished. Farhat returned to the accustomed spot to await his Princess's return. By and by she came, and under his eager guidance inspected all the miracles he had lovingly wrought. Anoush laughed like a child at the pretty things he had made for her, and gloried in the view from the topmost chamber. But then a petulant frown clouded her beautiful features. "There are no trees, or flowers, or fountains," she complained. She needed greenery around her, she said; and so, with her sweetest smile, she entreated Farhat to bring water to her palace and make the barren mountainside bloom. So saying, she rode away.

Once again Farhat enthusiastically set to work, his energy renewed by the sight of his beloved. He traveled to faraway mountains in search of brooks and rivers that he could divert from their courses, bringing them together in one mighty stream. To carry the waters over the intervening wastelands, he fashioned intricately engineered conduits and stately viaducts spanning deep valleys. On the hill itself, exquisite fountains and cunningly artificed basins received the precious liquid, leading it a brimming dance down through the palace's many terraces and galleries. And wherever the water went, Farhat laid down fertile soil

81

in irrigated beds, and planted trees and flowers to line its banks. He made vast hanging gardens that seemed to hover airily over the plain below, and planted them with rare seeds culled from the farthermost recesses of the land.

In time the trees grew and flourished, the flowers blossomed and spread, and the palace was filled with the sweet, heady perfume of exotic plants. The once-empty halls were brightened by the pleasant chatter of birdsong and the plash of falling water. Once more Farhat kept his lonely vigil by the rock, and although the tale of his labors was the table talk of the entire kingdom, this time his love did not come.

One day, as he sat chin in hand by the roadside, a peasant approached him along the desert track. The man was singing merrily; behind him trotted a donkey laden with provisions. Seeing Farhat, the man saluted him, then sat down to rest. Indifferently, the sculptor asked him where he had come from. A banquet, the traveler explained, trying to still the hiccups that kept on interrupting his speech. The King of Armenia was getting married, and he had been serving at the tables. The festivities had run on for seven days and nights; he had been able to load up his donkey with

enough surplus food and wine to last his family for a whole month.

Farhat thought of his own longed-for betrothal, and asked who the King of Armenia was marrying. A Persian Princess, the man replied, adding that news must travel slowly in the desert if he did not know of it, for their courtship had been long, and little else had been talked of in the towns. The bride was a great beauty, he explained. Then he added jovially, "Her name is Anoush."

Farhat sat dumbstruck while the tipsy traveler wavered off once more along the desert road. He thought of the smiling vision that had first won his love. He thought of the two interviews he had had with her, and of the promises that he had read into the Princess's words. He thought of the long years of backbreaking labor that had created the glorious palace now lying like an empty shell behind him. Then, with a despairing cry, he made his way to the topmost chamber and flung himself from its casement onto the rocks far below.

Soon the watercourses he had made dried up, and the flowers withered. Wind and dust eroded the fine carvings and embellishments of the palace, leaving it gaunt and crumbling. In later days, hostile armies invaded Armenia and used the palace as a prison for the native people. Time and decay continued to gnaw at it, until finally all trace of its once-great halls and terraces was wiped away. But the hill itself remained, a monument to the futility of unrequited passion.

A Warlock's Comeuppance

No mortal, in any station of life, was immune to the pangs of lovesickness. The passion to possess another could inflame a slave as easily as a scholar, a peasant as readily as a Princess. And few were better equipped to satisfy their longings than wizards and warlocks, who had all the tricks of the Devil at their command. Yet the tale was told, in the Scottish Lowlands, of a he-witch whose ploys did not succeed in quite the way he had hoped.

All the villagers of Saltpans knew that the schoolmaster John Fian was as learned in the dark arts as he was in Latin grammar. Nor did it escape their notice that he cast an amorous eye at every fresh-faced village maid. Those he could not seduce by sweet words, he bent to his will by spells and charms.

One day he pressed a young scholar, possessed of a pretty sister, to help him gain the maiden's favors by magic means. Fearing John Fian's wrath, the boy did as he was directed. He crept into his sister's bedchamber at midnight, to steal three red-gold hairs from her head. John Fian wished to use them in a love charm.

But the sister woke and caught him. She grabbed her brother by the wrist, and slapped him until he confessed his mission. Then, in consultation with her mother, who knew more about such matters than pleased the neighbors, the intended victim devised a trick. The little boy was sent to school the next morning, carrying three red-gold hairs wrapped up in paper. He did not know, and so could not reveal, that the strands did not belong to his sister, but to the well-fed young heifer his mother was rearing for market.

The mother and daughter folded their arms and sat back to wait. They knew that at the end of the day's lessons John Fian would hurry back to his own chamber to work his magic upon the hairs. He might choose to fold them up in a parchment inscribed with arcane symbols, or he might burn them in a candle's flame, all the while murmuring spells that would make their owner ache for love of him.

That afternoon, the two women heard lowing and stamping in the cowbyre. John Fian's spell appeared to be taking effect. The cowshed door had been left, by chance or design, off the latch. The agitated heifer soon nosed it open, and trotted off down the village street.

The beast stopped outside John Fian's door, moaning and snorting. When the schoolmaster emerged to drive it away, it turned on him and pursued him down the road, from the schoolhouse to the inn to the church and back again. Sometimes it raced ahead to present its hindquarters, as a cow would to a bull.

For weeks thereafter, John Fian had no peace. When he tried to drill his pupils, the cry of the lovesick heifer drowned out the lessons. When he went to church, the beast had to be forcibly restrained from pursuing him down the aisle; the wizard was the laughing stock of the entire district. Eventually the power of the charm waned, but by that time the wizard had learned his lesson. He realized how the girl and her mother had tricked him, and he now knew better than ever again to magic a maiden into submission.

When a Scottish warlock attempted to seduce a maiden by magic, his efforts went awry. Tricked by his intended victim, the charm that was intended to arouse her lust for him worked its powers on her heifer instead. He found himself pursued all over the village by the lovesick animal.

An Ill-Starred Mating of Earth and Sea

Deities and demigods could suffer the pangs of love as bitterly as mortals. They were as vulnerable to passion's grip and as liable to acts of folly. An old Japanese legend recorded how love blossomed between two divine beings from different spheres, and how the violation of a single taboo destroyed it.

Prince Howori was a hunter descended from the sun-goddess and the mountain god. From his youth, his chief joy had been the pursuit of deer and boar among the mountains his father ruled. When Howori reached manhood, his father gave him a magic bow that sent every arrow to its target. Howori's elder brother jealously noted this mark of favor. Fearful of losing his rights as the firstborn, he drove Howori from the crags and valleys he loved. Unable to withstand his brother's malevolence, Howori made his way to the seashore and scanned the horizon for a ship to bear him out of danger. Beside him, out of nowhere, appeared a man clad in seaweed and shells. To Howori's amazement, this unknown personage knew all about the brothers' quarrel. He had come, he explained, to offer Howori divine protection, since right was on his side. Howori watched as his mysterious benefactor cut down a clump of bamboos and wove the stems into a compact, seaworthy craft. He set it on the waves and Howori leaped in.

When he was far from shore, the sea began to churn, and Howori found himself in the center of a whirlpool whose waters sucked his boat beneath the surface. He descended through the depths and at length came to rest on the ocean bed before a palace.

Soon a young woman emerged. Her long black tresses floated all around her oval face. Strings of pearl and coral adorned her smooth white neck. But, as Howori approached the entrancing creature, she immediately took fright and ran indoors. In her place there appeared a stately old man who inquired the name of the stranger who had put fear into his daughter Toyotama. Howori introduced himself as the grandson of the sun-goddess, whereupon the older man announced himself to be the God of the Ocean and warmly invited Howori to stay in the palace as his guest.

Howori had fallen under Toyotama's spell, and before long he asked for and won her hand in marriage. The couple lived together in great joy. Their nights were filled with passion and their days idling con-

tentedly in the rocky bowers of the ocean floor. But sometimes Howori felt homesick for mountains, sky and snow, and occasionally he yearned for new faces. Of his bride's family, only Toyotama and her father possessed human form; her three brothers bore the shape of sea dragons.

Soon Toyotama told her husband that she was expecting a child. Howori, longing for home, persuaded her to bear it on dry land and live with him there. Toyotama agreed, but on one condition—he was not to see her again until after their child was born. He was to build a little house on the shore and thatch it with cormorant feathers. There she would come in her own time and give birth.

Bemused, Howori took tender leave of his wife. His father-in-law embraced him and placed in his hands a casket containing two jewels whose magic would protect him if his brother still bore the ancient grudge. One controlled the rising tide, the other its ebb. Climbing onto the back of a compliant dragon, one of Toyotama's kin, Howori traveled upward through the dark waters.

The monster deposited him on the seashore. Howori walked for many hours, reveling in the scent of the warm earth and the song of the birds among the cherry blossoms. At last he found his brother; looking into his sibling's eyes, Howori saw hatred burning as strongly as ever.

Howori blessed his father-in-law for his foresight and held one of the sea-jewels to his brow. Immediately the ocean broke its bounds and rose to engulf trees, fields and houses. The waters rushed up the hillside, parting to leave Howori bone dry. His brother shinned up a tall pine, but still the waters rose, until the tree was half submerged.

Clinging precariously to the topmost branches, the frightened youth begged his brother for mercy. Recognizing that he was now the master, Howori raised the second jewel. Immediately the ocean subsided. The elder Prince left his refuge and stood cringing before the mighty lord of the tides, ready to make peace.

His thoughts now turning to his wife's request, Howori chose a sheltered site on the seashore, built a hut and thatched it with cormorant feathers. Then he waited for many lonely

weeks. At last, one evening he heard a splash and the soft crunch of footsteps on the wet shingle, and he knew that Toyotama had arrived.

About midnight, her labor cries began. Howori pictured her alone, frightened and in pain. He buried his head in his arms and wept. For hours he suffered without moving, afraid to disobey her injunction. Then anxiety overcame him. He crept to the hut and peered through the window.

Through her birth agony, Toyotama sensed a presence. She looked round and saw her husband's face gazing in from the darkness. Her eyes widened in horror and she gestured wildly for him to leave. Shamed, he spent the rest of the night pacing his garden, trying not to listen to her screams.

At dawn, silence fell. Howori turned toward the hut and his heart froze. Slithering down the shore was a great sea dragon, its scales glinting in the sun's rosy beams. The monster launched itself into the sea, then dived and vanished.

Howori understood what had happened. The dragon was his beloved wife, whose human form had been lost through his disobedience. By ignoring the taboo on watching her in childbirth, he had destroyed both his own happiness and hers.

But as he gazed wretchedly at the vast ocean, he heard a whimper behind him. He searched for the source of the noise and among the tall reeds that grew in thick clumps at the shore's edge he found a newborn boy—a parting present from Toyotama.

True Love Triumphant

In the old chronicles, love often came to a joyous conclusion, but only after its subjects had suffered. Ritual ordeals, of perils and forced partings, were necessary rites of passage before a union was deemed worthy to endure.

The commonest trial was a separation. Sometimes the lovers were sundered by the edict of a hardhearted parent, desperate to avert a match that brought neither gold nor glory. In other stories, the painful severance might be brought about by the fortuitous arrival of a band of pirates bent on kidnap; by one partner's own weakness and folly; or by the machinations of an enemy—human or otherwise—who, through envy or less fathomable motives, wished the couple ill. In the most terrifying tales, the lovers were driven apart by death. But so powerful was love that it could vanquish even this grim adversary. Legends from opposite ends of the earth told of heroes who pursued the beloved even beyond the grave, and brought their mate back once more to the land of the living.

The accounts of these struggles taught, above all else, that love was far more than a mere convergence of lust and liking. It was an elemental force within the universe, the inspiration for great deeds, the impetus for poetry, the driving force of life itself.

The Soldier and the Saracen Maid

When Aucassin and Nicolette first set eyes on each other across a dusty Provençal market square, they were entranced. Gray-eyed Aucassin stood tall and strong. Nicolette possessed every grace known to woman. But, as the medieval troubadour who recounted the couple's tale explained, one major obstacle prevented their union: Aucassin was the only son of a great French lord, and Nicolette a Saracen girl captured in the Holy Wars.

Count Garin, Aucassin's father, ruled the city of Beaucaire in the land of Provence, and it was to Beaucaire that Nicolette had been brought as a prisoner. She had been baptized a Christian and reared in the household of the Viscount of the town, Count Garin's vassal, but she could never make a suitable spouse for the heir to Beaucaire.

When Aucassin informed his father that he wished to marry Nicolette, he was greeted at first with derision and then with consternation. He was told that he might pick from the noblest ladies of the realm. But Aucassin was stubborn. Failing to prevail with words, the Count sent orders that Nicolette be locked in a tower in the Viscount's palace. He forbade Aucassin all further contact with the girl, and warned that his soul would sojourn in hell to the end of time if he made Nicolette his mistress.

Then to hell he would go, Aucassin hotly replied. Heaven, he said, must be a sorry place indeed, full of old priests and pious cripples. Hell, though, sheltered bold knights, minstrels, troubadours and courtly ladies who had taken lovers. He would willingly be of that company, if he could have Nicolette by his side. So saying, he retired to his chamber and refused to come out, even when the troops of Count Bolgar of Valence, his father's neighbor and fiercest rival, invaded the lands of Beaucaire.

Things went badly for Count Garin, and before long the enemy was besieging the city of Beaucaire itself. Count Garin was too old and feeble to take the field, and ordered Aucassin to lead the army against the enemy. Instead of obeying forthwith, Aucassin bargained. Even in his great need, the old Count refused to countenance marriage between his son and Nicolette, but eventually he promised to allow one final meeting.

Aucassin was transformed by joy. With the aid of his squires and pages, he arrayed himself in his finest suit of mail. Then the gates were thrown open and Aucassin sallied forth at the head of his men. War cries and the thunder of hooves filled the air, and naked steel glittered in the bright Provençal sun.

In the cavernous solitude of Aucassin's iron helmet, the sound of his breathing drowned out the din of battle; the world seemed very remote. Aucassin dreamed of Nicolette and how she would admire him if she could only see him so magnificently attired. His charger, meanwhile, carried him deep into the enemy ranks, where he was quickly surrounded. Someone tore off his helmet, and a cry of exultation went up when he was recognized. Aucassin's reveries vanished. In a sudden frenzy, he drew his sword and laid about him like a

In battle, Aucassin was an unwilling knight.

man demented. In a short while he had unhorsed ten knights and wounded seven.

As he wheeled his charger to make his escape, Aucassin sighted Count Bolgar himself galloping across the battlefield. The Count did not see the great horse and mail-clad rider descend upon him, but only felt the impact. With a mighty clang he fell to the ground. Count Bolgar's men fled in disarray.

Aucassin brought his prisoner before Count Garin. While everyone rejoiced, Aucassin's only thought was of the bargain he had struck with his father. When he reminded him of his pledge, however, the Count stonily denied ever having made any promise. Aucassin reeled; for a moment he could not credit his ears. Then, gravely, he turned to his prisoner and offered him his freedom, without so much as the smallest ransom, on condition only that he never again attack Beaucaire. After his initial bewilderment, Count Bolgar readily assented and was escorted to safety by Aucassin. For this perverse deed the young knight was thrown into the castle dungeon on his return.

news of these events reached Nicolette in her tower, and her heart grieved for her beloved. She resolved to escape and thus spare him more suffering; once she was gone, he would surely be released. That night, she knotted her sheets together and slid down from the high windows of the tower. Hugging the shadows, she made her way to a spot in the city wall where siege damage had yet to be mended. Clambering over the loosely piled boulders, she reached the ditch beyond and scrambled with difficulty across it. Then she hurried across the fields to hide in a nearby forest.

Fearful of bears and wolves, she slept fitfully and rose early. As she plunged deeper into the woods, it struck her that if Aucassin were released, he would come searching for her, in which case he would need clues to help him. So when she came across some boys grazing their flocks, she made certain that they saw her pass. And when she arrived at a glade where seven paths converged, she built an arbor of flowers and branches that Aucassin would recognize as her handiwork.

Soon enough, news reached the castle that Nicolette had disappeared. Count Garin at once released his son and prepared a feast in his honor. But Aucassin was in no mood for feasting; he ran to his horse and set off in search of Nicolette. He hurried through the forest, looking for signs of her passage, until at last he came across the shepherds, who told him of the beautiful girl they had seen.

With fresh hope spurring him on, Aucassin made for the spot where they had glimpsed her. He rode all day and much of the night, and at last came to the arbor that Nicolette had fashioned. At first Aucassin was puzzled by the sight; then, in a flash, he realized it was just the sanctuary his love would build for shelter in the woods. Sure enough, she was waiting nearby. In his eagerness to embrace her, Aucassin stumbled and fell as he dismounted from his horse; Nicolette cradled his head in her lap as she gently massaged his bruised shoulder.

Barred from courtship, Aucassin met his love, Nicolette, in secret.

No one knows how long the lovers tarried in the bower, for the chronicle discreetly falls silent before the fulfillment of their happiness. But in that bird-haunted glade, heavy with the scent of lilies and of roses, their union was finally consummated and they became in their own eyes man and wife. For food, they had the plentiful nuts and berries of the forest; they drank the pure water of brooks. Their days were spent exploring the thickets and glades, where Aucassin kept a hunter's eye open for unwary deer or rabbits; their nights passed in lovemaking under the starlit boughs.

Finally the season began to change, and cold and the fear of hunger drove them from their woodland retreat. With Nicolette perched before him on the saddle, Aucassin rode away from the site of their happiness, trusting fate to steer the two of them toward good fortune. For days they traveled over parched plains and through hilly lands shaded with olive groves, finally emerging on a ridge overlooking the sea.

They galloped down to a beach of soft sand fringing a wide bay. A square-sailed merchantman was standing out from the shore. Aucassin waved and shouted to attract the attention of the mariners, who presently put a boat out to find what the strangers wanted. Passage overseas, Aucassin replied; and when he was asked where they were bound, he said it was no matter. Soon they found themselves aboard ship, heading for the open sea.

Within hours of their embarcation, powers beyond any mortal understanding took a hand in their lives. A curtain of darkness formed along the horizon; above, the clouds skittered as if in terror across the sky. For a while, the boat was becalmed in an eerie stillness; the sailors crossed themselves, knowing worse was to come. Soon the sun was blotted from the sky, and from the north came a terrible wind, which shrieked about the masthead like the souls of the damned.

The storm drove the ship before it for many days, taking it far off course into regions well beyond the range of the captain's charts. When the wind at last dropped, an unfamiliar shore loomed on the horizon. The ship steered for refuge to the first port sighted, and the two lovers made their way ashore into a land totally unknown to them.

Travelers in the old times often told of wonders, but few found lands that were stranger in their ways than the country of Torelore, to which the boat had been blown. It was a country, Aucassin found, in which knights were unknown. Seeking to earn his keep as a mercenary, he was directed to a town where, he was told, a battle was under way. But the combatants, it turned out, had neither pikes nor swords nor lances; instead they fought with whatever weapons came to hand: sticks, bottles, even rotten fruit.

For a moment, Aucassin wondered if he had lost his wits, then he laughed aloud at the bizarre spectacle confronting him. Expecting to win praise and fortune, he drew his own well-tempered blade and plunged into the fray, lashing out to right and left of him and spreading death and

In Torelore, wars were fought with rotten fruit and cheeses.

injury in his wake. To his further astonishment, though, men of his own side quickly restrained him and, taking away his sword, led him to their ruler. Killing for conquest was not the way of Torelore, the monarch explained; there, the people chose to settle conflicts without inflicting mortal injury.

Bemused by a country whose customs were so different from his own, Aucassin would no doubt soon have chosen to move on had he not been unhappily prevented. The lands surrounding Torelore were less humane in their attitude to the taking of life, and many individuals in them were only too happy to take advantage of their neighbors' military unpreparedness. Just two or three nights after the couple's arrival, a group of marauders attacked the capital while everyone slept. Before any warning could be given, they fell upon the town, hacking and hewing the unwary inhabitants with their cutlasses until the streets ran with blood. Those who looked young or fair enough were taken as slaves or concubines.

Aucassin and Nicolette were sleeping peacefully in one another's arms when the pirates burst into their chamber. Aucassin had no chance to reach for his sword before he and his love were seized and dragged off through the burning streets to the harbor. There Nicolette was forced into a boat whose cargo was young women. Aucassin howled in anger and struggled to fight free of his captors as they were separated; but a stunning blow from a cutlass hilt sent him reeling, and when he came to, it was to find himself manacled in the hold of a dark and creaking galley, lit by a single, swinging oil-lamp whose feeble glow was reflected in the bright eyes of rats.

From the deck of her boat, Nicolette watched the vessel to which Aucassin had been dragged bearing away toward the horizon and thought that fate had dealt her its last and cruelest blow. But further surprises were in store. The storms that swept the seas off Torelore had not finally abated. Soon the winds were again howling from a darkened sky, scattering the pirate fleet. Tossed and driven in their separate ships, Aucassin and Nicolette abandoned hope, and prayed the sea would quickly make an end of them.

But such was not to be their fate. After many days as the storm's plaything, the vessel that carried Aucassin was finally flung ashore, breaking up on half-submerged rocks. Aucassin was pulled from the wreck more dead than alive, only to find to his amazement that his rescuers were men of Beaucaire. The storm had carried him home.

His rescuers were quite as pleased to discover his identity as he was to see them. In the months that he had been away, Count Garin had died, leaving the land without a liege. The young knight returned as heir to his father's estates, and as soon as he had recovered from his ordeal, the nobility of the lands gathered to swear fealty to him.

In this way, Aucassin became Count of Beaucaire. He governed the land well, but the vivacity and lightheartedness of his youth were gone. He grieved sorely

Captured in a pirate raid, Nicolette was parted from her lover.

for his lost love, and wondered ceaselessly whether she was still living.

In fact, her story was even stranger than his own. She had been carried to the pirates' home port of Cartagena, in Muslim Spain. The skyline of minarets and domes that met her eyes seemed strangely familiar. Then the truth dawned. She had lived in this city as a child, brought up in luxury as the daughter of its ruler. From here the Christians had carried her captive to Beaucaire.

The pirates were doubtful when they heard Nicolette's story, but agreed to take her to the palace. There the monarch recognized her as his long-lost child. Embracing her with tears of joy, he commanded a feast in her honor.

Installed once more in the palace, Nicolette was spoiled and cosseted by her adoring father, but his constant care and gifts of clothes and jewels were tempered by a growing concern for her future. She must marry, he warned her; and when she showed no interest in any of the suitors who presented themselves, his solicitude turned to anger. He told her that if she refused to favor any of them, he would make the choice for her.

Nicolette, who had no thoughts for any man but Aucassin, made a show of accepting his decision; but in secret she laid plans to escape. She acquired a viol, and spent long hours with court musicians learning to play it. By night, while her handmaidens were sleeping, she altered the beautiful gowns that her father had given her. By day she combed the woodlands in search of a certain herb she had heard tell of; crushed into an unguent, it had the power to darken the skin.

A day came when, at her father's behest, Nicolette's betrothal to a wealthy neighboring potentate was announced. That same afternoon, a young, smooth-faced minstrel with a nut-brown complexion strolled out through the palace gates and down to the port. By the time she was missed, Nicolette was on a northbound ship. It was the beginning of a long and hazardous journey. Many nights she spent in rough taverns, singing for a platter of bread and cheese and a bed of straw. Her days, from the first bells of prime to evening vespers, were spent on the road until at last she reached Beaucaire.

Learning that her beloved Aucassin was now Count, Nicolette decided not to declare herself immediately. Instead she retained her disguise and, making her way to the castle, sat on a staircase and began to sing. Her voice was so pure and the melody so sweet that at length Aucassin came out of his chamber to listen. The gentle melancholy of the tune stirred half-suppressed memories, but his reverie was interrupted when he suddenly heard the name of his lost love. Nicolette, the minstrel sang, had been separated from her beloved by pirates, and had been taken to a foreign land; she had escaped, dressed as a minstrel, to find her way to the land where he lay.

At that moment Aucassin's eyes were finally opened. He married Nicolette the very next day, and for the rest of their lives they were the happiest Count and Countess that Beaucaire ever had.

The words of a minstrel's song led Aucassin to his lost lady.

Rescue from the Underworld

Love, said the poets, could conquer even death itself. In Polynesia, tribal storytellers handed down the tale of a young South Sea Islander who used cunning to rescue his beloved from the spirit world.

Its hero was a youth called Hiku, who lived with his mother in a cavern high on a volcanic peak. One day he left, to roam the island wilderness below. There, in a distant village, he met and fell in love with a lowland chieftain's daughter named Kawelu. The two lived together happily for a time. But Hiku had promised his mother to return; filial duty eventually tore him from his new love's side.

Months later, he made his way back to Kawelu's village. He found that she had pined away with grief and, just days before, had died. In his anguish, Hiku sought to redress the wrong he had done Kawelu and to be reunited with her. He knew her spirit would have gone to the underworld. He knew, too, where that was to be found, for his mother had often spoken of it. Gazing out from their mountain aerie far across the blue ocean, she would point to the horizon line, where the sky came down to meet the water. There, she said, lay a great abyss, in which the spirits of the dead dwelled.

All the islanders knew of the place, and most looked forward to going there, for it was a world without sorrow; but no living man dared approach it, since it was fiercely guarded. In his despair, Hiku vowed to undertake the perilous venture. He knew it would be no easy matter to tempt Kawelu back to the land of the living. And so he devised a ruse.

First he wove a long rope from thick vines. At one end he fixed a wooden crossstick, thereby fashioning a swing of a type every islander knew and had played on. Next, he split a coconut and hollowed out each half. Then, he coated his body with rancid coconut oil. The foul stench mimicked the smell of corpses, a trick to deceive the guardian of the dead.

Accompanied by Kawelu's kinsmen, Hiku set out by canoe for the great chasm. At its edge his companions steadied the canoes and lowered him on the plaited rope over the verge of the abyss.

Down he went until he was within the sight of the watching shades. Then Hiku began to swing. In ever-increasing arcs, he swept back and forth above the assembled spirits; as he did so, happy memories of their lives on earth assailed the gazing throng. None was more moved than Kawelu, who recognized her lost lover. Eagerly, she leaped up to join him.

Hiku signaled to his friends to haul in the rope. At first Kawelu was too absorbed in play to realize what was happening, but when she did, panic gripped her. Using the shape-shifting powers of the dead, she transformed herself into a butterfly to fly back to the underworld.

But Hiku was prepared. He clapped the two coconut halves around her fluttering form and carried her back to the world of the living. Returning to the village where her corpse lay, he made a small incision in the body and coaxed the butterfly-spirit back to its earthly home. Kawelu stirred into consciousness, and she and her rescuer were never parted again.

Clinging to a plaited vine, the Polynesian hero Hiku descended to the place where the dead dwelled, a chasm beyond the horizon. He sought to rescue his love, who had languished and died for want of his company.

Travails of an Indian Queen

In earlier days, the lore of every land was replete with lovers who, like Aucassin and Nicolette, struggled prodigiously to attain their goal of wedlock. But in India, the tale-spinners also paid tribute to a different kind of devotion: the loyalty of a wife to her wedded husband. In the Indian fables, set amid wild forests and scented palace gardens, steadfast women suffered indescribable privations and terrors for the sake of their wayward mates. The flower of these faithful wives was Damayanti, consort of King Nala.

From its beginning, Nala's courtship of Damayanti was marked by marvels and the intervention of otherworldly beings. Ruler of Nishadha in northern India and a superb horseman, Nala possessed the highest qualities of a man and a King. His only fault was a love of dice which some called immoderate. Damayanti was the treasured daughter of Bhima, Raja of the nearby state of Vidarbha. For beauty and sweetness, she outshone every woman. The fame of such creatures naturally spread far, and their interest in each other had quickened before they ever met.

Increasingly obsessed by thoughts of the girl, Nala took to roaming silently among the flowering trees of his garden, where one day he surprised a flock of swans with golden wings. He caught one of them, and to his amazement it promised in a human voice that, in return for freedom, it would plead his cause with Damayanti. Duly released, the swan and its fellows flew at once to the garden at Vidarbha, where Damayanti and her maidens were idling in the shade. The girls sprang up and chased the birds all

Nala, a lovesick Indian Prince, sent a swan to plead his cause with
the lady Damayanti. Landing in Damayanti's garden, the bird
lured her away from her handmaidens to deliver its entrusted message.

over the garden. When Damayanti cornered her quarry, the swan urged Nala's suit. Silenced at first by wonder, she collected herself enough to bid the bird convey her tender feelings to Nala.

Thereafter Damayanti became pensive and pale, losing her appetite for life. Everyone could guess what afflicted her, and her wise father decided that the time had come for Damayanti to choose a husband. Bhima therefore invited all the greater lords to attend his court. They swarmed to Vidarbha from far and wide, each one vying to outdo the others with the splendor of his entourage. Among them traveled Nala.

As he galloped along, Nala was suddenly brought up short by four radiant gods, who dropped from the blue air before him. They informed him that they, too, coveted Damayanti, and they enjoined Nala to be their spokesman. He begged to be excused such a painful service, but they insisted—and his piety made him obey. The gods spirited him into the Princess's bower, where he scrupulously carried out his commission.

But the moment that Damayanti saw Nala in the flesh, her heart went out to him alone. Realizing this, the four gods joined the other prospective bridegrooms who had gathered to await Damayanti's choice. To confound the poor girl, each of the celestial beings assumed a form identical to Nala's. Wise in the ways of her world, where gods walked often, Damayanti understood the game that her divine suitors were playing. And by scrutinizing the five identical petitioners, she began to perceive the small but certain

signs of godhood: Four of the quintet cast no shadows. They did not sweat, their eyes were unblinking and their feet barely hovered on the ground.

Recognizing her true beloved, Damayanti joyfully placed a garland around his neck to indicate her choice. They solemnized their union by walking around the sacred flame that was symbolic of fidelity.

When the Prince led Damayanti around the sacred nuptial fire, it seemed as if their match was smiled upon by all the gods. But a jealous demon, thwarted in his own designs upon the bride, was already plotting to blight their union.

As a wedding gift, the gods, magnanimous despite their defeat, charged the bridegroom with supernatural powers: These included culinary wizardry and the strength to overcome fire.

And so the lovers were united, but their very happiness made them an implacable enemy: A certain demon had also wanted Damayanti as his bride, and in his jealous chagrin he swore that he would humble the great Nala, however long he had to wait to do it.

Unaware of their doom, the couple dwelled together in peace, beloved by all their people. In time, two beautiful children were born to them, a boy and a girl. Nala's attachment to games of dice sometimes cast a shadow over his wife's happiness, but for twelve years she banished her worries, trusting her husband to discipline his weakness.

Then came a fatal day when one small unthinking error on Nala's part gave the demon just the chance he had been waiting for. The Raja failed to wash his feet before going to his prayers, thereby giving offense to the gods. At once the demon slipped like a ferret into his soul and took possession of it.

The demon's stratagem for bringing Nala to destruction was to inflame his fondness for gambling into an uncontrollable passion. Summoning Nala's brother Pushkara, who had gazed long on Nala's good fortune with covetous eyes, the demon promised Pushkara that he would win whenever he threw dice with the King, for an evil spirit would enter the dice and govern how they fell.

Nala was utterly powerless to resist the desire within him. Day and night, month after month, he played on, deaf alike to the pleas of his beloved Damayanti and to the remonstrations of his most trusted counselors. Nala lost every game he played, and each loss cost him a possession. Fearful of what the future held, Damayanti sent the children to safety in her father's palace.

Nala forfeited his treasures, his palace, his kingdom. At last his brother proposed with a cruel smile that they should play one more game, for Nala's last remaining treasure: for Damayanti herself. In grief and horror Nala rose up. Silently he laid aside his rich garments, and went out humbly clad in the single cloth of a beggar. Behind him followed the sorrowing figure of faithful Damayanti, clad too only in a loincloth.

Their wanderings and their hardships were terrible, for the new Raja Pushkara forbade the people to give Nala and Damayanti any succor. They were finally forced to seek refuge in the wild forest, searching for roots and berries to keep themselves alive.

Tormented by guilt and racked with remorse, Nala pained Damayanti greatly by continually urging her to leave him, and pointing out the road to her father's city. Fiercely she refused, insisting that she would stay to offer him the comfort of her love. But one night, while Damayanti slept, Nala stole quietly away and left her, prompted partly by shame and partly by the demon who still dwelled malignantly within him.

Damayanti's grief and distress on finding herself so cruelly abandoned were at first too much for her to bear. But even when she had recovered herself, she did not, for a moment, think to reproach the husband who had deserted her. The fears she felt as she stumbled on through the dark and menacing forest were only for Nala, not for herself. Although many dangers came near her—wild beasts, demons, evil and violent men—her purity and unearthly beauty preserved her from all physical harm.

It was many days before the Princess, her garment now ragged and filthy, her hair torn and dust-streaked, came to the royal city of Chedi, which glittered in a great clearing of the forest. Her strange

Despite all his virtues, Nala possessed one fatal weakness. He gambled compulsively, staking ever more of his domains and fortunes on the toss of the dice.

Emerging from the forest into a royal city, the half-clad Damayanti endured the mockery
of a jeering mob. But the Queen spied her suffering from the palace, and succored her.

appearance attracted the attention and then the mockery of a jostling crowd. She was only rescued from their impertinences by a messenger from the mother of the city's King, who had spied Damayanti from the roof of the palace where she was strolling. The Queen could tell from Damayanti's bearing that she was of gentle birth, and she welcomed her with kindness and inquired about her plight. Damayanti would not say who she was but, reassured that she would be treated as befitted her rank, she agreed to stay as companion to the Queen's daughter.

Here Damayanti lived while her father Bhima made ceaseless efforts to discover what had befallen his luckless daughter. The Brahmans that he dispatched to seek her visited every known city, until at last one of them found his way to Chedi. In spite of the marks that her suffering had left upon her beauty, the Brahman recognized Damayanti as she stood beside the royal ladies. He told them her identity and without delay they arranged to convey her home to her father's palace, where she was welcomed with tearful rejoicing. Once her story was told, her father turned his efforts toward locating the missing Nala.

When the unhappy King left his sleeping wife, he had rushed deeper into the forest. Suddenly a great ring of fire blazed before him; from its center he heard a voice calling him by name and begging for help. Using the power over fire that he had received from the gods at his marriage, he leaped unharmed through the circle of flames and found a giant serpent trapped at its center. Conquering his awe and terror, Nala questioned the creature. The serpent, Nala learned, was Karkotaka, demigod King of snakes, and he had been imprisoned within the wall of fire for deceiving a holy man.

Karkotaka promised to reward Nala fully if he would carry him to safety. When they emerged from the flames, the serpent bade the King walk forward ten steps. At the tenth, Karkotaka bit him, instantly transforming his strong straight body into an ugly, twisted shape. The snake hastened to explain to Nala that the change was for his own benefit, so that he could pass unrecognized.

The serpent-king instructed Nala to seek employment as a charioteer to the Raja Rituparna of Ayodha. This Prince was a mathematical genius and consummate dice player. He was also well known as a horse lover, but he was clumsy in his handling of the beasts. Nala might find an opportunity to impart his own skill with horses, the snake suggested, and could ask the Raja in return to share his invaluable knowledge of dice. Finally, the snake gave Nala a magical robe that would restore his original form when the right time came. Then the serpent-king vanished from sight.

Nala did as he was bidden. His skill with the horses impressed the Raja Rituparna, who made him chief of all his drivers and heaped honors upon him. Nala's shame, however, weighed on him ceaselessly. He could not be comforted.

At the same time, far away in his own capital, Damayanti's father again sent Brahmans to every quarter of the land, giving them all a message to utter a verse begging the wandering gambler to return to the wife he had deserted as she slept in the wild wood. At length an envoy returned from Raja Rituparna's court to report that he had received a response. A deformed charioteer had seemed much moved by the words, and had called on the woman to earn merit by remaining constant, never yielding to anger against the husband who deserted her, robbed as he was of his kingdom and his happiness.

The message convinced Damayanti that her husband had at last been found. She divined, however, that he was still too torn with shame to approach her, and that she must apply all her wit to bring him to her side once again. She sent another emissary to Raja Rituparna with the message that Queen Damayanti was about to select a new husband. The messenger added that if the Raja wanted to contend for her hand, he must complete the long journey to Vidarbha in a single day, for the choice would be made at dawn on the morrow.

Immediately the Raja sent for his charioteer, the only man who could drive the distance in a day. When he heard the Raja's orders, Nala's anguish was intense, for he thought Damayanti must have given him up for lost. But he promised to do the Raja's bidding and, as soon as his master was aboard the chariot, urged the steeds to give their utmost. Like an arrow, the chariot flew forward.

The Raja yearned to kindle fire in the horses like Nala, and ached to master the foaming team himself. Struck by a happy thought, he reminded his driver of his own pre-eminent knowledge of the rules of chance, which enabled a man always to win at dice. He proposed that they should trade the secrets of their arts. The charioteer agreed, and reined in so that they could do so immediately.

Aghast, the Raja protested that they could not possibly spare the time. "Proceed without me if you wish," taunted the charioteer, and the Raja, defeated, imparted without delay the secret key of numerical knowledge. As the wisdom of the dice entered Nala's mind, the light of understanding drove forth the demon, freeing him from its grasp.

Immediately the driver sprang back to the chariot rail, and they flew on to reach Vidarbha by evening. The thunder of the horses as the chariot whirled into the palace courtyard put Damayanti in mind of Nala. Her heart filled with ecstasy.

The misshapen driver whom Damayanti observed from her terraced roof looked as different as could be from the godlike Nala. Yet, as Damayanti watched him hobble into the servants' quarters, she sensed that she beheld her husband. To confirm her intuition, she sent her most trusted maid to repeat to the charioteer the verse that the Brahmans had used to seek Nala. The maid reported back to her mistress the emotion with which he made his answer, in the same words as before. Then Damayanti instructed the maid to purloin a spoonful of the supper that the charioteer was cooking for himself. As soon as Damayanti tasted the ex-quisitely spiced meat, she knew that the dish was the creation of her husband, with his god-given culinary skills. Finally she sent her two children to greet the charioteer; the maid recounted how he had gasped at their approach and embraced them, moved to tears.

Then at last Damayanti requested her parents to summon the strange man to her. Weeping, she asked him if he knew anything of Nala, that great King who had so inexplicably deserted his faithful wife. At that, Nala abandoned the fiction that he was not her husband, and spoke to her directly. He explained how his foolish and cruel acts had been beyond his control, inspired as they were by a demon. He reproached Damayanti for proposing to choose a second husband.

Swept by emotion, she revealed that her announcement had been a stratagem to bring him to her, and solemnly swore that she had remained pure. Convinced of her honesty, Nala wrapped himself in the magic robe the serpent-king had given him, and so regained his manly form.

Amid great rejoicing, husband, wife and children were reunited. Nala honored his promise to Rituparna by imparting to him his knowledge of horses, and it remained only for him to win back his possessions and titles from Pushkara. With the knowledge of the dice that he had received from Rituparna, it took him only one throw to regain all. He forgave his astounded and alarmed brother, and welcomed back to her rightful place his faithful dark-eyed Queen. Thenceforth the royal couple lived in love and virtue among their devoted subjects.

The enchanter's snare

Those who despaired of fair dealing in love might find hope in the lay a medieval poet sang of a Breton couple's fortunate deliverance. Arveragus and his lady Dorigen were so enamored that even the briefest parting was torture. When Arveragus was sent by his lord on a mission to England, Dorigen refused to be consoled. Day after day she paced the cliffs, gazing at the jagged rocks below and imagining her beloved shipwrecked before he could return to her arms.

One morning, a young squire of her acquaintance named Aurelius fell into step beside her and confided that a passion for her had long burned in his breast. Dorigen replied without pause that she would never betray her husband. Then she jestingly qualified her abrupt refusal. She would welcome Aurelius' embraces, she declared, on the day he rid the coast of Brittany of its treacherous rocks.

Tortured by his love for Dorigen, Aurelius turned to an astrologer famed for creating illusions more real than life. Aurelius offered a princely sum if the sage could make the rocks of Brittany disappear for a week. The learned man calculated the conjunction of the planets most favorable for his magic. At the due hour, the Brittany coastline seemed to flatten into perfectly smooth, sandy curves. When Dorigen next glanced from her window, she was dumbfounded. With horror, she recalled her promise.

That night, Arveragus returned home. Dorigen told him all. The knight declared that since the very foundation of their marriage was honesty, she must keep her word to the squire. Afterward, Arveragus would accept her back. When Aurelius learned of this exchange, he was so moved by Dorigen's distress and by her husband's nobility of mind that he at once relinquished his claims. And the astrologer, not wishing to be outdone in chivalry, waived his fee.

Deathless Devotion

During the long, cold evenings of a Tibetan winter, storytellers would recount the tale of a couple whose love was strong enough to survive not only parental opposition but even death itself. The pair, whose names have been lost with the passing of time, met at a ford. Each day, they would make their way there separately to bring their families' yaks to water, and one morning they fell into conversation. They stayed talking for a long time and parted unwillingly, agreeing to meet again the next morning. And by the time of that second encounter, they were in love.

The weeks that followed were anxious ones for the couple. Marriages in old Tibet were family matters, often arranged at birth; unplanned unions were a source of shame. They had to hide their love from their families while hurrying each morning to meet one another at the ford.

A day came when the young man seemed more distracted than ever as he waited for his love to arrive; his whole body trembled when he finally heard the girl approaching. Hardly had they exchanged greetings before he revealed the secret that had kept him in such trepidation. He had brought for her a rich family heirloom, a silver earring inlaid with a large turquoise.

At the sight of the gift the girl fell silent, for she knew that to accept it would be an irrecoverable pledge of her love. Then, impulsively, she unraveled a

A young Tibetan herdsman pledged his troth to his beloved by plaiting an earring into her hair. She accepted both the gift and the trouble she knew it would bring.

braid, and allowed the youth to plait the earring deep into her long, black hair. At that moment, she resigned herself to take whatever consequences might ensue.

A daughter in the first flush of love cannot long hide her emotions from a mother's scrutiny, and the earring was soon discovered. Realizing at once the depth of her daughter's commitment, the older woman decided that only desperate measures could save the family's honor. She dispatched her eldest son to kill the interloper who had stolen the affections of her child. This command was not strictly obeyed, however. Her son had little heart for the task, and aimed his arrow only to wound the yak-herder. But unbeknown to him, she had taken the precaution of poisoning the arrowtip; in anguish, the young man died.

The girl was overcome with grief and decided on a course of action that would relieve her from her misery forever. Winning permission from her father to attend her lover's funeral, she hurried to the ceremony to find the body already laid out on the funeral pyre. But try as they might, the young man's family could not get the pyre to catch fire.

Approaching the kindling, the girl took off her cloak. To the astonishment of the other mourners, she cast the garment onto the wood, which at once flared up. Then, with a howl of woe, she

*Refusing to endure life without her murdered
lover, the girl flung herself on his
funeral pyre before the eyes
of the startled mourners.*

hurled herself onto her lover's bier, and amid the crackling flames the two were consumed together.

The onlookers stood aghast at the horror they had witnessed. Word of the tragedy quickly traveled to the girl's mother, who hurried to the scene. Arriving in all her fury before the last embers of the conflagration had had time to cool, she resolved that the young couple should not be allowed to remain united even in death, and insisted that their bodies, which had become fused together in the fire's heat, be separated.

The mourners sent for a local shaman, who sought to know what the two lovers had been most afraid of in life. The girl, it transpired, had always loathed frogs; the lad had a terror of snakes. So a snake and a frog were duly caught and let loose near the burned corpses. At once, the bones miraculously leaped apart. Then, at the mother's insistence, the two piles were buried on opposite banks of the river, so that the lovers should be kept asunder for all eternity.

Soon, however, two saplings sprouted from the newly dug graves. With unnatural speed they grew into spreading trees, their branches stretching out and intertwining across the stream. To the passersby it seemed as though they were reaching to embrace one another, and children playing nearby reported fearfully that the enlaced limbs sounded like the whispered words of lovers.

Angrily, the mother commanded the trees to be cut down, but each time the woodchopper's ax laid them low they sprang back up again. So, in a way that no one could have foreseen, the two managed to show their devotion, and their love continued to flourish even after death in the soil of their graves.

From the lovers' graves grew two great trees. Like longing arms, their branches reached toward one another and clung together, resisting any effort of weather or wind to part them.

Of a Knight and his Lady Lost

In a church in the province of Artois on the borders of France, there lay the effigies of a knight and a noblewoman, side by side, their stone elbows touching. The statues marked the tomb of the warrior Sir Eglamour and the Lady Chrystobel—two who suffered long and bitterly for the sake of their love. The history of their ordeal and its final resolution is a tale of wonders and prodigies spanning many years and many lands.

Sir Eglamour was a knight in the service of Count Frensamour of Artois. His misfortune was to fall in love with gray-eyed Chrystobel, the daughter of his master. He could hardly aspire to win her hand in marriage; the proud, possessive Count dismissed even suitors of royal blood.

But his desire for her, inflamed by secrecy, tormented him by day and possessed his dreams by night. At the sound of her footfall on the cold flags of a corridor, at the smallest glimpse of her shadow gliding over a wall, his heart raced and the blood thundered in his brain. When at night the court assembled to feast, Sir Eglamour would lean back in his chair and stare past the other diners at Chrystobel. Then his stomach would clench like a fist and he would push his plate away from him in despair.

At length he fell ill with love. That night, a chair stood empty at the baron's table. Frensamour sought to know which of his knights was absent. On learning that it was the bold young Eglamour, whose exploits in the lists he had admired, he solicitously asked his daughter to find out what ailed him.

Chrystobel slipped away, hiding a blushing smile, for the handsome young man's attentions had not escaped her notice. She made her way to his chamber, where she found him listlessly sprawled on the bed. The sight of Chrystobel at once revived him. He declared his love for her in words of fierce passion, swearing he would die if she did not heed his suit. When he at last desisted, Chrystobel's smile told him all he needed to know. Demurely she said that she would speak of him to her father, and suggested that Eglamour should approach him after the lists on the following day.

The sun had set, risen, and was going down again when Eglamour, on his Gascon stallion, galloped up to the Count. The last joust was over, and Frensamour, jaded and dissatisfied with the day's sport, was preparing to ride back to court. Eglamour hailed him. Then, before the whole court,

the young knight dismounted and begged Frensamour for his daughter's hand.

Horses fretted in nervous sidesteps in the long silence that followed. Eglamour's friends among the riders waited in dread. But the Count at last favored Eglamour with a smile. It would, he said, be an honor to embrace him as a son-in-law; the whole court knew him for a gallant and noble knight. He must first, however, perform three small services as proof of his worth. He must seek out and fight to the death the forest ogre known as Maroc; then hunt down and slaughter the giant boar that terrorized the land of Satyn. Finally, he must kill the dragon that menaced the city of Rome. So saying, Frensamour rode off, laughing into the wind.

He had charged Eglamour with a mission of honor that the young knight could not refuse. But the adversaries he had chosen were so fearsome that no mortal man could expect to survive the encounters. Undaunted, Eglamour remounted and, turning to the castle, raised his sword in salute. From some window, he knew, Chrystobel would be watching. Then, without further delay, he set off to face the first of his ordeals.

After many days Eglamour came to the territory of Maroc. Here, in the dark heart of the forest, nothing moved. No bird sang; no breeze stirred the trees. Eglamour stopped and waited. Suddenly, a pair of mighty elms flew apart before him. Maroc, three times larger than any normal man, strode out, wielding a club the size of a young tree.

Eglamour drew his sword. From where the elms had parted, a shaft of sunlight struck the polished blade and dazzled Maroc with its brilliance. Bellowing in his blindness, the giant stumbled. Eglamour, darting in close, rammed his sword into Maroc's throat, slit it from ear to ear, then hacked off the head.

His first task accomplished, Eglamour went in search of the great boar of Satyn. The forest all around its lair was littered with the mangled remains of hapless dogs and men that had met with the beast while coursing.

Eglamour stalked his quarry by moonlight, armed with a spear. The boar ran from him all night, but as dawn broke, it turned on its pursuer and charged. Eglamour aimed his weapon straight between the boar's tusks, but the beast's skull was so thick that it buckled the point. Flinging the useless spear away, the knight fell upon the animal with his sword and stabbed it through the heart.

Many days later, Eglamour, proud in victory, stood before Count Frensamour with two grisly trophies. Frensamour scowled and tapped the table angrily, but concealed his emotions as he addressed the knight. Congratulating him on his successes, the Count reminded him that a third task remained. The dragon of Rome was the plague and despair of that city. It would be a service to its citizens to destroy the monster. Patting the knight's arm in a travesty of paternal affection, Frensamour dismissed him, first graciously granting him twelve weeks' rest.

The time that followed was the happiest of Eglamour's life. His days were filled with hunting, his nights with feasting, and everywhere that he went the reputation of his feats preceded him; he was received with admiration and respect. Best of all, he had the love of Chrystobel. In public, they maintained a facade of decorous courtship. In private, though, they met often, at a secret trysting-place deep in a nearby forest.

The idyll sped by, and at the end of the twelve weeks Eglamour took ship for Italy after giving his lady a gold ring as a pledge of his troth. Ahead of him lay the most terrible task of all. The dragon was the very soul of ferocity, as Eglamour could plainly see when he approached the woods where it lived. What had once been lofty aspens and cedars were everywhere charred to stumps. The earth was scoured and scorched black. The monster devoured whatever crossed its path, blasting its prey with hurricanes of flame.

Eglamour faced the creature with stoic courage. He flung himself at his adversary, his sword flashing in wild circles above his head. The dragon, grown indolent with years of easy conquest, was taken off guard. In a second, Eglamour had struck off one of its wings, then a leg. Stunned and crippled, the dragon backed away and spat a crackling ball of fire at its assailant. Deflecting the flames with his shield, Eglamour ran in again and jammed his sword into the dragon's mouth. With a roar of pain, the beast reared up, lifting the knight in its jaws far up in the air. Then it flung him down on his back. His body ripped and broken, Eglamour lay gasping for breath and, through a thickening veil of blood, watched the dragon of Rome die. Rumors of his victory quickly spread to the city, and before nightfall a deputation of courtiers arrived to rescue the stricken knight. He was taken to the ruler's palace and received as a hero. But his wounds were many and deep, and were slow to heal. For months, the knight lay bedridden, trapped between life and death.

Far from her lover, Chrystobel in Artois had more than his absence to fret over; she had discovered that she was carrying his child. For as long as she could, she tried to conceal the secret, binding herself tightly in linen to hide the truth even from her maids. Inevitably, the news leaked out, and soon afterward, she gave birth to a fine son.

The Count was consumed with rage. His little girl, his pride, now seemed a treacherous child-whore nursing a retainer's bastard. To salve his honor, he resolved to kill them both. Yet even Frensamour could not bring himself to slaughter mother and child in cold blood. Instead, he bundled them into an old fishing boat, rudderless and rotten, and set it adrift, leaving his weeping daughter and grandson to the mercy of the waves.

Yet in this plan, too, Count Frensamour was thwarted. The brittle timbers of the keel let water in, but, miraculously, the old boat did not sink. Pitching and yawing, it swept along for a week or more before striking the reefs that fringed a peninsula. The old hull finally split asunder, but Chrystobel and the child were thrown onto a bleak shore. There, shivering in the dark, Chrystobel rocked the baby to sleep and listened to the waves hurling themselves against the land. She heard, too, another rhythm: a sound as of great wings beating laboriously overhead.

When morning came, bleeding gray light across the jagged rocks, she saw to her amazement that something was indeed hovering above her. It was no ordinary bird, but a griffin—a winged beast with the head of an eagle and the body of a lion.

As she gazed open-mouthed, the monster plunged down and snatched her baby away in its talons. Chrystobel screamed, but with a rush of wings the griffin rose again and swept toward the horizon.

Her home, her love and now her baby had all been torn from her. Yet Chrystobel's plight was not as terrible as it then seemed, for what she did not and could not know was that, in their fearsome journey south, she and her child had crossed an invisible line into the realms of magic, where things deemed impossible in Artois could and did occur.

Her baby did not die. The griffin carried him not to some mountain aerie, but to the court of its keeper, an old Levantine King. The kindly monarch had long sought an heir. Receiving with joy the child dropped miraculously from the sky, he named him Degrobel and swore to raise him as his son.

Fortune took pity on Chrystobel too. After weeks of wandering over lonely heights and desolate plains, she was discovered by merchants traveling home to Egypt with a spice caravan. A wild and disheveled figure she seemed to them, but through the disorder of her dress and her rambling speech they sensed nobility in her bearing. So they laid her down gently in a covered wagon and, when they reached their destination, took her to their King. He too received her kindly. Though already the father of several daughters, he welcomed Chrystobel into his home and treated her as one of his own.

So it came about that, through the unfathomable workings of fate, the three victims of a father's cruelty all found themselves in foreign courts, ignorant of one another's whereabouts. Eglamour, still fired by hope, was the first to make a move. But when he finally rode back into Artois, it was only to learn of Chrystobel's presumed demise.

For a time his fever returned, and in his delirium he raved of plans to kill the Count. With restored health, however, came resignation; robbed of the chance of happiness, Eglamour resolved to take the cross and set off for the Holy Land.

Time passed, some sixteen years or more, before the last act of the star-crossed lovers' strange destiny was finally played out. The King of Egypt sought to seal a treaty with a neighboring monarch by means of a diplo-

matic marriage, and of all the women of his court, Chrystobel was to be the chosen bride. Sorrow had bred indifference in her, and to please her benefactor she consented to the arrangement without demur. When the visiting party arrived, she scarcely glanced at her intended husband, until she noticed the emblem on his helm: a griffin with one foreleg clutched around an infant, as though to guard it. A wild thought crossed her mind, hardening into certainty as he offered her his hand; for on it she saw a ring—the very one Eglamour had given her many years before. She had hung it around her baby's neck, to serve as proof of his noble birth should they become separated.

Joy and anguish flooded through Chrystobel's mind. But before she could speak to the young man, a flourish of trumpets sounded in the castle yard, proclaiming to the world the banns of marriage, and announcing the beginning of a tournament in which the groom would joust against all comers.

It so happened that Sir Eglamour was in Egypt at that time. The crusade was over and, fatigued and lonely, he was making his way slowly back to Artois. Like many other ex-crusaders, he engaged in prizefighting to pay his way. Hearing the invitation from afar, Eglamour rode into the tournament and, as was a stranger's right, took his place among the other contestants.

So it was that Sir Eglamour rode against his own son on his wedding day before the eyes of his long-lost love. How the older knight unhorsed the younger, then chivalrously raised him from the ground; how Chrystobel recognized the victor as he raised his helmet in salute; how she shocked the crowd by running into the lists to embrace the stranger—these were for many centuries the themes of tale-tellers' narratives and minstrels' songs.

When the two rulers presiding over the tournament learned, in breathless snatches, the strange truth, they vowed at once to help right old wrongs. With their blessings, Sir Eglamour and Chrystobel, separated for the best years of their lives, were finally united in matrimony. Degrobel, too, had cause to rejoice, for now he was free to marry his own love, Ardanata, daughter of the King of Satyn. For years the pair had loved each other in secret, but had despaired of enjoying any future together, knowing that Degrobel's fosterparent intended him for a more strategic match. Now there was no impedi-ment to their union. A joint wedding ceremony was held for the two couples: Mother and son walked to the altar together to clasp the hands of their chosen mates.

Thus it came about that the love of Eglamour and Chrystobel triumphed against all odds. When the festivities were over, the couple returned with their son and daughter-in-law to Artois. There Chrystobel's father, Count Frensamour, still ruled. The bitter disappointments of his past, the certain prospect of dying without heir, made him even more arrogant and spiteful than he had been in his prime. If he suffered any remorse for dispatching his daughter and grandchild to the doubtful mercy of the waves, he had never confessed it.

It was said that he became a tyrant to his subjects, and a martinet within his court. He passed his days devising laws that increased the misery of the populace. With the connivance of venal stewards, he raised the taxes on his tenants and peasants, and took pleasure in witnessing the confiscation of their chattels, goods and livestock when they could not meet his onerous demands. His dungeons became overcrowded with those who had, by word or deed, displeased him, and his black-hooded executioners were busy.

Some say that Count Frensamour, spying their approach from a high tower, was struck down by fear and guilt and tumbled to his death; others claim he was slain by Sir Eglamour in a duel. Fireside history recalls only that the noble Sir Eglamour became King of Artois and Chrystobel his Queen, and that for the rest of their lives they were content to spend much time alone together.

139

Acknowledgments

The editors wish to thank the following persons and institutions for their help in the preparation of this volume: Guy Andrews, London; Mike Brown, London; Lesley Coleman, London; Fergus Fleming, London; The Folklore Society, London; John Gaisford, London; Nick Growse, Bury St. Edmunds, Suffolk; The London Library, London; Jackie Matthews, London; Kate Pullinger, London; Deborah Thompson, London.

Picture Credits

Bibliography

Ahmad Shah, Rev.:
   Four Years in Tibet. Benares: E.J. Lazarus & Co., 1906.
   Pictures of Tibetan Life. Benares: E.J. Lazarus & Co., 1906.
Aldington, Richard, and Delano Ames, transl., *New Larousse Encyclopedia of Mythology.* London: The Hamlyn Publishing Group, 1985.
   The Arabian Nights' Entertainments. London: George Routledge and Sons, no date.*
Ashton, John, *Romances of Chivalry.* London: T. Fisher Unwin, 1887.*
Aston, W.G., *Shinto, (The Way of the Gods).* London: Longmans, Green and Co., 1905.
   Aucassin and Nicolette, and Other Tales. Transl. by Pauline Matarasso. Harmondsworth, England: Penguin Books, 1971.*
Baker, Margaret, *Discovering the Folklore and Customs of Love and Marriage.* Aylesbury, England: Shire Publications Ltd., 1974.
Baldick, Robert, *The Duel.* London: Chapman and Hall, 1965.
Ballard, Martin, *Scholars and Ancestors; China under the Sung Dynasty.* London: Methuen Educational Ltd., 1973.
Barber, Richard:
   The Reign of Chivalry. Newton Abbot, England: David & Charles, 1980.
   The Knight and Chivalry. Ipswich: Boydell Press, 1974.
Boyajian, Zabelle C., *Armenian Legends and Poems.* London: J.M. Dent & Sons Ltd., 1916.*
Bulfinch, Thomas, *Myths of Greece and Rome.* Harmondsworth,

England: Penguin Books, 1981.*

Cavendish, Richard, ed., *Man, Myth and Magic*. 11 vols. New York: Marshall Cavendish, 1983.

Chandler, Richard E., and Kessel Schwartz, *A New History of Spanish Literature*. Baton Rouge, Louisiana: Louisiana State University Press, 1961.

Christie, Anthony, *Chinese Mythology*. Feltham, England: The Hamlyn Publishing Group Ltd., 1968.

Coghill, Nevill, *Geoffrey Chaucer, The Canterbury Tales*. London: Penguin Books, 1951.*

Cotterell, Arthur, and Yong Yap, *The Early Civilization of China*. London: Weidenfeld and Nicolson, 1975.

Davis, F. Hadland:
Myths & Legends of Japan. London: Harrap & Company, 1912.*
Japan, From the Age of the Gods to the Fall of Tsingtau. London: T.C. & E.C. Jack Ltd., 1916.

Davis, William Stearns, *Life on a Mediaeval Barony*. New York: Harper & Brothers, 1923.

Delort, Robert, *Life in the Middle Ages*. Transl. by Robert Allen. London: Phaidon Press Ltd., 1974.

Ellis, George, *Specimens of Early English Metrical Romances*. London: Henry G. Bohn, 1848.

Gernet, Jacques, *Daily Life in China on the Eve of the Mongol Invasion 1250-1276*. Transl. by H.M. Wright. London: George Allen & Unwin Ltd., 1962.

Gibson, Michael, *Gods, Men and Monsters from the Greek Myths*. London: Peter Lowe, 1977.

Givry, Grillot de, *Witchcraft, Magic & Alchemy*. Transl. by J. Courtenay Locke. New York: Dover Publications, 1971.

Goodrich, Norma Lorre, *The Ways of Love*. London: George

Allen & Unwin Ltd., 1965.

Gower, John, *Confessio Amantis (The Lover's Shrift)*. Transl. into modern English by Terence Tiller. Harmondsworth, England: Penguin Books, 1963.

Grene, David, and Richmond Lattimore, eds., *Euripides*. Vol. IV of the Complete Greek Tragedies. Chicago: The University of Chicago Press, 1958.

Grigson, Geoffrey, *The Goddess of Love*. London: Constable, 1976.

Guerber, H.A., *Legends of the Rhine*. New York: A.S. Barnes & Co., 1895.*

Gupta, Shakti M., *Loves of Hindu Gods and Sages*. Bombay: Allied Publishers, 1973.

Herald, Jacqueline, *Renaissance Dress in Italy 1400-1500*. London: Bell & Hyman, 1981.

Hogarth, Peter, and Val Clery, *Dragons*. London: Allen Lane (Penguin Books), 1979.

Hope Moncrieff, A.R., *Classic Myth and Legend*. London: The Gresham Publishing Company, 1912.

Hull, Eleanor, *Folklore of the British Isles*. London: Methuen & Co. Ltd., 1928.

Hyde-Chambers, Fredrick and Audrey, *Tibetan Folk Tales*. Boulder, Colorado: Shambhala Publications, Inc., 1981.*

Kalakaua, His Hawaiian Majesty, *The Legends and Myths of Hawaii*. New York: Charles L. Webster & Co., 1888.

Lane, Edward William, *Arabian Society in the Middle Ages*. London: Chatto and Windus, 1883.

Leach, Maria, ed., *Funk & Wagnall's Standard Dictionary of Folklore, Mythology and Legend*. San Francisco: Harper & Row, 1984.

Leyel, Mrs. C.F., *The Magic of Herbs*. London: Jonathan Cape Ltd., 1920.

Lha-Mo, Rin-Chen, *We Tibetans*.

London: Seeley Service & Co., 1926.

Lines, Kathleen, ed., *Faber Book of Greek Legends*. London: Faber & Faber, 1973.*

MacCulloch, J.A., *The Childhood of Fiction: A Study of Folk Tales and Primitive Thought*. London: John Murray, 1905.

Macfie, J.M., *Myths and Legends of India*. Edinburgh: T. & T. Clark, 1924.*

MacKay, Dorothy Epplen, *The Double Invitation in the Legend of Don Juan*. Stanford University, California: Stanford University Press, 1943.

Mackenzie, Donald A., *Indian Myth and Legend*. London: The Gresham Publishing Company, 1913.*

Mandel, Oscar, *The Theater of Don Juan*. Lincoln, Nebraska: University of Nebraska Press, 1963.

Mardrus, Dr. J.C., *The Book of the Thousand Nights and One Night*. Transl. by Powys Mathers. London: George Routledge & Sons, 1947.*

McClelland, I.L., *Tirso de Molina*. Liverpool, England: Institute of Hispanic Studies, 1948.

McNeill, F. Marian, *The Silver Bough*. Vol. 1 Scottish Folk-Lore and Folk-Belief. Glasgow: William Maclellan, 1957.

Meller, Walter Clifford, *A Knight's Life in the Days of Chivalry*. London: T. Werner Laurie Ltd., 1924.
Ovid, *The Metamorphoses*. Transl. by Henry T. Riley. London: Bell & Daldy, 1869.*

Owen, D.D.R., *Noble Lovers*. London: Phaidon Press Limited, 1975.

Page, Robin, *The Country Way of Love*. Harmondsworth, England: Penguin Books, 1983.

Parker, Alexander A., ed. by Terence O'Reilly, *The Philosophy of Love in Spanish Literature*. Edinburgh: Edinburgh University

Press, 1985.

Pasteur, Violet M., *Gods and Heroes of Old Japan.* London: Kegan Paul, Trench, Trübner and Co., 1906.*

Piggott, Juliet, *Japanese Mythology.* Feltham, England: Newnes Books, 1982.

Pindar, *Pindar's Victory Songs.* Transl. by Frank J. Nisetich. Baltimore, Maryland: The John Hopkins University Press, 1980.

Ramsey, Lee C., *Chivalric Romances.* Bloomington: Indiana University Press, 1983.

Rank, Otto, *The Don Juan Legend.* Transl. by David G. Winter. Princeton, New Jersey: Princeton University Press, 1975.*

Rigg, J.M., transl., *The Decameron of Boccaccio.* London: The Navarre Society Limited, 1921.*

Riordan, James, *A World of Folk Tales.* London: The Hamlyn Publishing Group, 1981.*

Sanders, Tao Tao Liu, *Dragons, Gods & Spirits from Chinese Mythology.* London: Peter Lowe, 1980.*

Scherer, Margaret R., *The Legends of Troy in Art and Literature.* New York: The Phaidon Press, 1963.

Seaton, R.C., *Apollonius Rhodius, The Argonautica.* London: William Heinemann, 1912.

Seklemian, A.G., *The Golden Maiden and Other Folk Tales and Fairy Stories told in Armenia.* Cleveland, Ohio: The Helman-Taylor Company, 1898.

Sharpe, Charles Kirkpatrick, *A Historical Account of the belief in Witchcraft in Scotland.* London: Hamilton, Adams & Co., 1884.

Thompson, C.J.S., *The Hand of Destiny.* London: Rider & Co., 1932.

Thompson, Stith, *Motif-Index of Folk Literature.* 5 Vols. Bloomington, Indiana: Indiana University Press, 1968.

Thrum, Thos. G., *Hawaiian Folk Tales.* Chicago: A.C. McClurg & Co., 1907.*

Vickery, Roy, ed., *Plant-Lore Studies,* Mistletoe Series Vol. 18. London: The Folklore Society, 1984.

Walker, Benjamin, *Hindu World.* London: George Allen & Unwin Ltd., 1968.

Werner, E.T.C., *Myths & Legends of China.* New York: Benjamin Blom, Inc., 1971.

Westermarck, Edward, *Ritual and Belief in Morocco.* Vols. 1 and 2. London: Macmillan, 1926.

Williams, C.A.S., *Outlines of Chinese Symbolism and Art Motives.* Rutland, Vermont: Charles E. Tuttle Company, 1974.

Wilson, Richard, *The Indian Story Book.* London: Macmillan and Co. Limited, 1914.*

Titles marked with an asterisk were especially helpful in the preparation of this volume.

Time-Life Books Inc.
is a wholly owned subsidiary of

TIME INCORPORATED

FOUNDER: Henry R. Luce 1898-1967

Editor-in-Chief: Henry Anatole Grunwald
Chairman and Chief Executive Officer: J. Richard
Munro
President and Chief Operating Officer: N. J.
Nicholas Jr.
Chairman of the Executive Committee: Ralph
P. Davidson
Corporate Editor: Ray Cave
Executive Vice President, Books: Kelso F. Sutton
Vice President, Books: George Artandi

TIME-LIFE BOOKS INC.

EDITOR: George Constable
Executive Editor: Ellen Phillips
Director of Design: Louis Klein
Director of Editorial Resources: Phyllis K. Wise
Editorial Board: Russell B. Adams Jr., Thomas
H. Flaherty, Lee Hassig, Donia Ann Steele,
Rosalind Stubenberg, Kit van Tulleken,
Henry Woodhead
Director of Photography and Research: John
Conrad Weiser

EUROPEAN EDITOR: Kit van Tulleken
Assistant European Editor: Gillian Moore
Design Director: Ed Skyner
Chief of Research: Vanessa Kramer
Chief Sub-Editor: Ilse Gray

PRESIDENT: Christopher T. Linen
Chief Operating Officer: John M. Fahey Jr.
Senior Vice Presidents: James L. Mercer,
Leopoldo Toralballa
Vice Presidents: Stephen L. Bair, Ralph J.
Cuomo, Neal Goff, Stephen L. Goldstein,
Juanita T. James, Hallett Johnson III, Carol
Kaplan, Susan J. Maruyama, Robert H.
Smith, Paul R. Stewart, Joseph J. Ward
Director of Production Services: Robert
J. Passantino
Quality Control: James J. Cox

THE ENCHANTED WORLD

SERIES DIRECTOR: Ellen Galford
Picture Editor: Mark Karras
Designer: Lynne Brown
Series Secretary: Eugénie Romer

Editorial Staff for *The Lore of Love*
Text Editor: Tony Allan
Staff Writer: Ellen Dupont
Researcher: Susie Dawson
Sub-Editors: Frances Dixon, Jane Hawker
Design Assistant: Julie Busby

Editorial Production
Coordinator: Maureen Kelly
Assistant: Deborah Fulham
Editorial Department: Theresa John,
Debra Lelliott

Correspondents: Elisabeth Kraemer-Singh
(Bonn); Maria Vincenza Aloisi (Paris);
Ann Natanson (Rome).

Chief Series Consultant

Tristram Potter Coffin, Professor of
English at the University of Pennsylvania, is a leading authority on folklore.
He is the author or editor of numerous
books and more than one hundred articles. His best-known works are *The British Traditional Ballad in North America*, *The
Old Ball Game*, *The Book of Christmas Folklore* and *The Female Hero*.

This volume is one of a series that is based
on myths, legends and folk tales.

Other Publications:

FIX IT YOURSELF
FITNESS, HEALTH & NUTRITION
SUCCESSFUL PARENTING
HEALTHY HOME COOKING
UNDERSTANDING COMPUTERS
LIBRARY OF NATIONS
THE KODAK LIBRARY OF CREATIVE PHOTOGRAPHY
GREAT MEALS IN MINUTES
THE CIVIL WAR
PLANET EARTH
COLLECTOR'S LIBRARY OF THE CIVIL WAR
THE EPIC OF FLIGHT
THE GOOD COOK
WORLD WAR II
HOME REPAIR AND IMPROVEMENT
THE OLD WEST

For information on and a full description
of any of the Time-Life Books series listed
above, please write:
Reader Information
Time-Life Books
541 North Fairbanks Court
Chicago, Illinois 60611

Library of Congress Cataloguing in
Publication Data
The Lore of love.
   (The Enchanted world)
   Bibliography: p.
   1. Love — Folklore 2. Tales
I. Time-Life Books   II. Series
GR460.L67 1987   398.2'7   87-6519
ISBN 0-8094-5281-2
ISBN 0-8094-5282-0 (lib. bdg.)

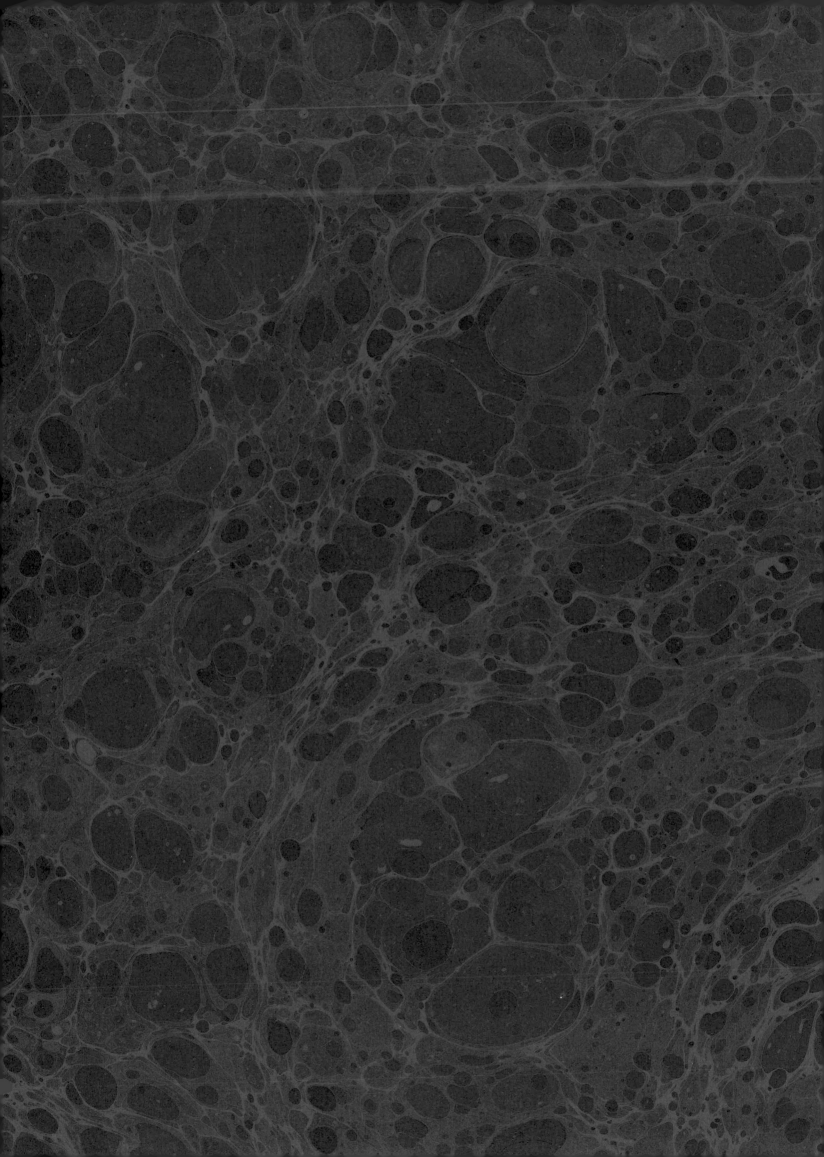